# ONLY HUMAN

Guide to our
internal Human Operating System
and Achieving a Better Life

NORBERT SOSKI

Straight-Up Soulutions, Los Angeles, CA

Library of Congress Control Number:  2018909977

ISBN: 978-1-5356-1443-6 (hardcover)
ISBN: 978-1-5356-1442-9 (paperback)
ISBN: 978-1-5356-1444-3 (ePub)
ISBN: 978-1-5356-1445-0 (mobi)

Learn more about Norbert Soski and his appearances at www.NorbertSoski.com

Printed in the United States of America

I dedicate this book to Marisa and Daniel, because the future depends upon role models like you.

And a special dedication to my rock, soul mate, best friend, and wife, Sharon; your strength and love gives me purpose and that has made all the difference in the world.

I also dedicate this book to the memory and lives of my mother and father, Helen and Joseph. People who (like many others) survived more in their lives than any woman and man should have to endure. My father, in light of all that, always said, *"If there's a will, there's a way."*

# I'm Only Human

by Anonymous

Dear Self,
You are only human.
You are *not perfect*,
and really if you were,
how absolutely dreadful that would be.

But Self, do remember,
that you are *not defined by your imperfections*,
you are not ruled nor controlled,
*merely challenged.*

Think of it this way,
you now have a chance to *be better than you were*,
you now have a chance to *understand more about yourself*,
people around you,
and the world as a whole.

So in essence what separates the wise,
from those who pretty much take themselves too seriously,
is *your reaction to yourself*.

*Lighten up.*
You're not all that bad.
You're actually really good.

So when you look in the mirror,
and notice all the blemishes,
smile and say,
*this too shall pass.*

After all,
you are *only human*.

Emphasis added by the author.

# CONTENTS

# INTRODUCTION

*There are two sorts of curiosity — the momentary and the
permanent. The momentary is concerned with the odd appearance
on the surface of things. The permanent is attracted by the amazing
and consecutive life that flows on beneath the surface of things.*
— Robert Wilson Lynd, Solomon in All His Glory

"I WANT, I WANT, I want"; that is the kind of behavior you would expect from a child.

I have always been a curious person. When I was a child, I took everything apart; my father's car radio, my sister's Barbie doll playhouse, the family television set, and the list of things goes on and on. I needed to know how all those things worked, and disassembling them led me to a better understanding of their parts and function. And if I wanted a toy or plaything, I built one on my own with stuff from around the house. Early on I used milk cartons, cardboard, and staples; later on, it was wood and nails, metal and screws. I built model submarines, toy tanks, soapbox cars, and many more big and small toys.

This all led me to the world of engineering as an adult. My parents would say to me ever since I was five years old, "You are going to grow up to be an engineer." I did not disappoint them. As an engineer, I have created toys for children, computers for satellites, electrical power for the space station, and engines for rockets. But my curiosity in general has also led me to look at other things, beyond the physical world of science.

Before I considered writing a book about human nature, I first struggled to understand the general behavior of people. For many years, I observed the people around me, trying to understand why they believed in certain things, performed certain behaviors, and said certain things (even when people exposed to the same experiences believed, did, and said different things). So much of what people did and said did not make "logical" sense, nor was it consistent with the events as I saw them. So, I undertook a personal study of the human condition. I avoided any individual characteristics that may be attributed to personality and looked for a universal set of characteristics that could be attributed to the greater group, human beings as a whole.

During my study of the human condition, I observed people as they went about their daily lives. And then when I noticed something interesting in their behavior[1], interaction[2], or response[3], I would evaluate the event and analyze the behavior to make sense of it. I used the engineering methods I had learned and have used throughout my career, to explore and understand the deeper meanings of my observations. Those observations, mixed with a little spirituality, have led me to a great appreciation and understanding of the human condition.

What kept coming up over and over again was the concept of "that's human nature." And that human nature exhibits itself in many forms. Most of us see our human nature like this:

- We are creatures of habit.
- We are not perfect; we all make mistakes.
- Accidents happen.
- We do not like change.
- We make excuses for our actions and inactions.
- We have the potential for inflicting great cruelty.
- We have big egos and are self-centered.
- We need to be right all the time.
- We can be very emotional and dramatic.

---

1 Behavior — the human being's overall response to stimulation or the environment.
2 Interaction — action with each other, reciprocal action or effect.
3 Response — reaction or behavior resulting from the application of a stimulus.

Some of the time, human nature is even invoked as an excuse for our failings — we use it like a "Get Out of Jail Free" card,[4] or "I couldn't do this, that, or the other thing [fill in the blank]. What do you want from me? I'M ONLY HUMAN!!!"

I decided to put my discoveries and thoughts in writing to share them with others and to see whether others get what I got. In this book, I make a bold effort to explore as much of human nature as I can and decipher this rarely understood subject and the often mentioned and maligned phrase "I'm only human."

Now it is time to open up on the subject and reveal the hidden causes of our human nature. I call this set of workings the internal Human Operating System (iHOS) because it precisely describes how we human beings operate.

Most people are completely blind to their own human nature. They delude themselves about reality because they simply ignore it or, worse yet, convince themselves that the very conditions of human nature do not apply to them or that they are immune to its effects. And yes, these people come from all walks of life and all levels of intelligence.

The bottom line is that human nature is real and we all experience it equally, and for us to be successful in life, we need to first understand it, then pay attention to it, and then, ultimately, interact with it correctly. Once we clear up the complexities, assimilating the detailed information in this book should take our thinking and behavior to a different level. You will look at life with more understanding. You will see human interactions from a different perspective. You will escape the make-believe world and start living in reality. You will know how to prevent human nature from running your life automatically

> *"The greatest discovery of my generation is that a human being can alter his life by altering his attitudes."*
> William James

---

4 Get Out of Jail Free card is a reference to the *Monopoly* game.

so that you can deal with what is "real." In most cases, this will give you an increased ability to interact with other people, which leads to greater success and happiness.[5]

We might say human nature is human nature — it is what it is. It's like the air we breathe; it's all around us. People also once said this about gravity, but detailed understanding and knowledge of the phenomenon of gravity has led to many further discoveries and creations, ultimately the travel to other planets. The same can be assumed about understanding human nature.

If you are not satisfied with your status quo, or if having a "bigger, better life" motivates you, any new information about you that can help you produce positive changes in your life is what you need, and that is what this book provides — a unique perspective on our human nature.

So many people have said in so many different ways that the definition of insanity is "doing the same thing over and over but expecting a different outcome." If you want something different in your life, then you must change how you do life. You can change some of the ways you perceive life around you. You don't need to make any more wish-lists or New Year's resolutions. Instead, you can alter your viewpoint on life — see it from a different perspective that is sharpened with new and better insights. Without this change, it will be more of the same, cycles of routines and similar results.

Note that this book is broken down into various parts, steps, and sections. Part 1 is the learning part (Sections 1, 2, and 3; Chapters 1 to 16):

- The first section (Chapters 1 to 3) provides an understanding of the human condition and our human nature. The objective of this section is to get you to appreciate the importance of

---

5 Happiness — is very much a personal issue. We each have different pictures of what it should look like. Happiness may have external influences: money, career and job, and accumulation of material things (house, cars, jewelry, clothes, and other toys). It also has internal influences: quality of one's relationships, attitude toward life, and level of suffering and pain. For the purpose of this book, success and happiness means obtaining the external and internal influences you need to have life go your way and get all that you want: having a life of fulfillment.

understanding our human nature and how it affects our lives, success, and happiness, and that of the entire world. This helps you understand why you need to read Section 2.

- The second section (Chapters 4 to 8) explains the internal Human Operating System and its characteristics. The objective of this section is to reveal the details about our internal Human Operating System so that you understand how it operates within us.

- The third section (Chapters 9 to 16) explores how our internal Human Operating System actually affects key areas of our lives. The objective of this section is to help you develop a true understanding of how our internal Human Operating System influences every part of life — every part.

Part 2 of this book is the action and improvement part (Section 4):

- The fourth section (Chapters 17 and 18) is where we learn about the twelve action steps and how to incorporate them into our lives. The objective of this section is to provide the tools and guidelines to help us adjust and gain control over our internal Human Operating System so we can experience more freedom and happiness in our lives.

Also included are exercise breaks to help you assimilate the new information and explore how the material presented affects your life directly. Please stop and take the time to complete these exercises because they help your learning experience.

It takes time to unlearn years of bad habits and, in some cases, core beliefs. But change we must so that we can make this a better world because *good* is not good enough. We all deserve more and better.

So we begin our journey into human nature. An engineer's perspective on human nature offers some unique perspectives. By taking this approach to discovering the secrets of our human nature, we can employ engineering processes and methodologies, such as reverse engineering and system modeling, to identify and resolve its complexities.

# Reverse Engineering and Modeling

When an engineer wants to understand how a completed product was made, the engineer goes through a process of reverse engineering. In reverse engineering, the engineer takes apart a finished product, piece by piece, top down, to get to the set of constituent parts. The goal of disassembling the product is to understand how it functions so as to duplicate or improve it.

When an engineer wants to create a new product, the engineer begins by understanding the physical principles and properties of the imagined product and then models those key characteristics to create a detailed picture of the product. This operational model allows the engineer to understand how the product functions under various conditions and in different environments. The better the operational model represents reality, the better the resulting product. From this detailed understanding, the engineer can fabricate a final product that complies with all its design and functional requirements.

In science, to discuss a major system, such as the universe, plate tectonics, or the weather, scientists develop operational models of the system. The operational model helps us understand the parameters and complexity of the system and theorize about its behavior in a way that can then be tested and used to forecast future states of the system.

Later on in the book, after reverse engineering the human being, I present an operational model of the human being. This model, called the Human Control System (HCS), provides us a deeper understanding and explanation of how human beings operate and how the concept of human nature works and fits in, and within the Human Control System is the internal Human Operating System that drives the Human Control System.

# Computers and Operating Systems

A computer (even a smartphone) is composed of two major parts: hardware and software. The hardware is all those components that are mechanical and electrical: the case, the display, the keyboard, the mouse, the hard drive, and the electronics inside the case. The software is the operating system and the application programs — executing within the electronics — that makes the computer do what we intend it to do.

Part of the electronic hardware is the central processing unit (CPU), often referred to as the "brains" of the computer. The software executes in the CPU. The computer hardware would just sit there and do nothing if it were not for the software.

A computer operating system (OS) is the software that manages all the computer hardware resources and provides common services for the application programs. The operating system brings life to the computer hardware; it makes the display light up and the hard disk drive operate. Most people are familiar with the different popular operating systems available today: Microsoft Windows, Apple OS X, and Linux.

Within the operating system are the device drivers, which handle the low-level operations of the computer hardware, such as writing text to the screen, reading the keyboard and the mouse, and accessing the disk drive memory. All the work performed by device drivers is hidden in the background. The application programs are totally unaware of their operations. The application programs simply direct that information be displayed on the screen or stored in memory, and the task is performed automatically by the device drivers.

Application programs are software programs that computer users (you) install on their computers so that the computer does what they want it to do. Each user determines the specific set of application programs to install on the basis of personal needs, such as word processing, games and music, or search functions.

## Robots and Control Systems

Robots and control systems are very similar; they each interact with the "real world" in some way, whether the robot is assembling an automobile in a factory or the control system is running a heating, ventilation, and air conditioning (HVAC) system in a home. These systems operate by taking in real-world parameters, such as air temperature, humidity, or piece-part positions, and then creating some desired result, such as comfortable air quality in a home or a brand-new car.

In general, control systems are stimulus-response mechanisms; meaning the control system monitors a predefined set of input sensors (stimuli) and calculates or processes some set of outputs (responses) based on the desired state of the control system and the set of input sensors.

An HVAC system in a home is an example of an interactive control system. In the HVAC system, a thermostat senses the temperature in the house and displays that information for you to know. Monitoring the house temperature, the thermostat turns the HVAC system on and off to keep the house at the preferred temperature. You can manually control the HVAC system, but in general it operates automatically to sustain the desired comfort levels programmed in.

## Change and Growth

Most people are trapped by their own beliefs[6] about themselves and about the world. These preconceived notions keep us from seeing the truth about ourselves, that is, who we appear to be to others. You may have been told once or many times that you are in some way or another displeasing and that you need to stop being that way. People might pick on something minor about your personality or something that, as far as you are concerned, is a fundamental characteristic that defines you. They may say you are:

> *"People don't want to hear the truth because they don't want their illusions destroyed."*
> Friedrich Nietzsche

- Always late (never on time)
- Disorganized, a slob

---

6 Beliefs — mental models, paradigms, assumptions, and/or biases.

- Mean and angry
- Indecisive (cannot make a decision to save your life)
- Pushy and overbearing
- Unfocused
- Obsessive compulsive
- Overweight, fat, unfit
- Self-centered, arrogant
- Pompous
- Too forgiving
- A poor listener

Then they might say you need to do something about it — "you need to change."

Most of the time, we respond to other people's suggestions about our alleged character flaws by ignoring them, telling them they need to mind their own business, or fighting back to defend ourselves. Somehow, justifying our character flaws or, worse yet, refusing to see or acknowledge them does not in any way affect our potential need to change any more than continuously watering a dead plant will bring it back to life.

> *"Yesterday I was clever, so I wanted to change the world. Today I am wise, so I am changing myself."*
> Rumi

Personal change is a touchy subject and unfortunately, resisting or avoiding change is part of our human nature (more on that subject later). When we take an honest look at our life, we may have said, "There is some room for improvement in my life, maybe just a little." The struggle we often have is with *how* to change in addition to what to change.

> *"Social revolutions and group revolutions are good, and we need that, but we also need personal revolution — revolution within ourselves that change who we are as people."*
> Ziggy Marley

How should we go about making changes? Willpower alone does not create change. Relying on willpower is like standing over a flat tire and yelling at it to change itself. In the end, the tire is still flat and you are exhausted. If we knew how to change, we might have already done so — I tried to change many times, but I just could not until I learned more about the mechanisms that drive us. To create meaningful and lasting change, we first need to know the mechanics of human nature.

When we change the way we see things, the things we see change. So change is important. Change is the movement from one condition to another condition. These conditions may have some dependence one on another. These conditions may or may not be better one to the other. All we know is change is change — we move from one set of beliefs and practices to another. Change gives the illusion of progress because each change brings us to a different place, but that new place may or may not move us toward improvement or an objective.

> *"Our dilemma is that we hate change and love it at the same time; what we really want is for things to remain the same but get better."*
> Sydney Harris

More powerful than just change is growth. Whereas change is the movement from one point to another, growth is change in a positive and useful direction, toward a goal or desired endpoint built on previous change (see Figure 1). You cannot have growth without change, but growth brings you to your goals.

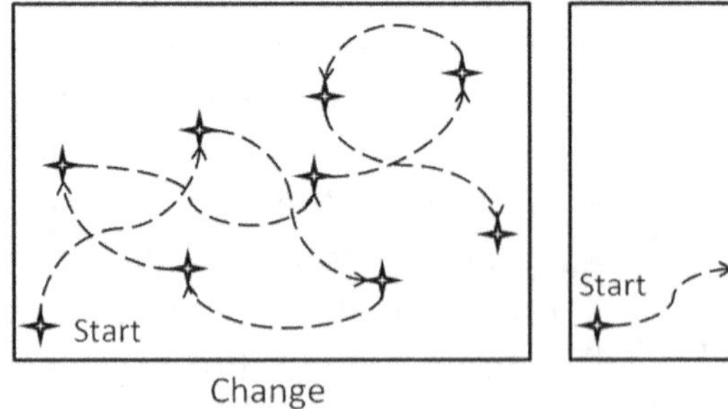

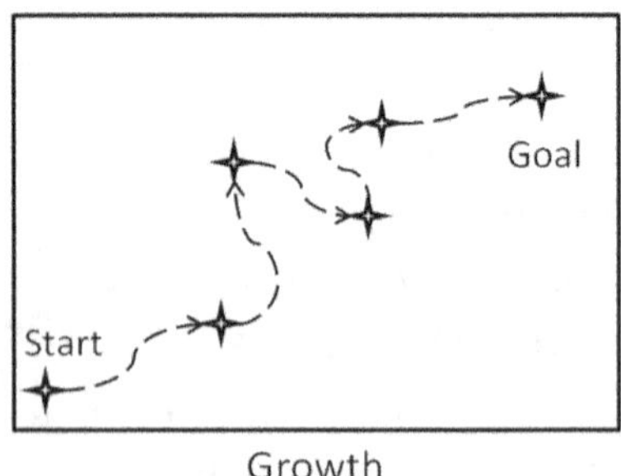


**Figure 1. Growth is better than just change.**
*Change is just motion with no real plan; growth is positive change with a clear path toward a defined and specific goal.*

Ultimately, we cannot change the world around us until we change ourselves first. We cannot fix the problems in Darfur until we fix our relationships[7] at home first.

## Exercise Break

Let's look at change, the need to change, and the reasons to change:

Step 1. Make a list of characteristics or circumstances in your life that you would like to change. Be as specific as you can; the more specific, the better. Here are some examples, I am...:

- Always late (never on time)
- Disorganized, a slob
- Mean and angry
- Indecisive
- Pushy and overbearing
- Unfocused
- Obsessive compulsive
- Overweight, fat, unfit
- Self-centered, arrogant
- Pompous
- Too forgiving
- A poor listener

Step 2. Now let us look at your desire or need to change. This is how much you want to be different tomorrow from how you are today. Regardless of whether you have tried to change before and failed, today is a new day. Write down your "becauses," whys, and reasons to change. Are you changing for you, your spouse (partner or significant other), your children, your dog, your health, your career and job, your success, or your happiness?

---

7 Relationships — people you have a connection with: parents, siblings, spouse, partner, or significant other, children, friends, neighbors, boss, and coworkers.

## I Can Because I Want To

There are two fundamental aspects to change and growth. The first is that we will not change and grow unless and until we want to, regardless of whether we need to. This bears repeating: we will not change and grow unless and until we want to, regardless of whether we need to. No one can make us do something we are unwilling to do or take us where we are unwilling to go. To change who we are, to grow into a better person, we need an acceptable "because," "why," or reason. In fact, we need a really compelling reason, because change is sometimes not easy or pleasant. To change, we may need to know (or really get) how painful the outcome of our behavior can be, and we have to really want to minimize the amount of stress, pain, and suffering in our life. The motivation[8] to change must be voluntary. It is about being a better person today and every day into the future.

> *"If it is important to you, you will find a way. If not, you'll find an excuse."*
> *Intervent Email*

Let me put it to you this way: if someone presented you with a new idea that was radical but promised to deliver the results you were looking for, and you had the option to take a chance on that new idea or ignore it and go on with your life as it is, would it not make sense to choose to believe in the new idea? That choice has some potential upside. I like to believe that we can teach old dogs new tricks, no matter the age of the dog. This book presents a new way of looking at life and human nature, and you might go along with it to grow into the life you want for yourself.

The second fundamental aspect of change and growth is that we cannot change or improve until we know how, which requires we know the truth about who we are. This is about discovering and better understanding human nature. When we are more aware of our

---

8 Motivation — some inner drive, impulse, intention that causes you to do something in a certain way toward some goal or purpose.

human nature, we can respond to situations and people in a more appropriate and effective manner. We also gain a better understanding of why people do and say what they do and say.

Imagine opening a box of parts for a Scandinavian-made bookshelf unit that did not come with any assembly instructions or even a picture of what the finished product should look like. Where and how would you begin to put it together? Even a picture of the end result or goal would be helpful, and assembly instructions would move assembly along even faster. That unmarked box of bookshelf parts is what change looks like when we go about it without an understanding of the pieces that make us up or how they fit together. Look at this book as your guide to our internal Human Operating System (iHOS).

## *Key Takeaways*

1. We know we need to change, but we do not know how to change. If we do not know what makes us do what we do, how can we change what we do?
2. This book can help us develop two important abilities:
   a. The ability to understand other people and to know why they do what they do
   b. The ability to understand ourselves and to know why we do what we do.
3. It is now time to do something different — to change and grow as a person — so that we can create a better future.
4. There are two fundamental aspects to change and growth:
   a. We will not change and grow until or unless we want to, regardless of whether we need to. We need a compelling reason.
   b. We cannot change or grow until we know how, which requires we know the truth about ourselves; otherwise, we do not know where we are starting from or how to make the necessary changes.

5. On the journey to understanding human nature, we must be willing to take the first step and every step thereafter. We must be willing to go the distance.
6. This book is your guide to our internal Human Operating System (iHOS).

# THE HUMAN CONDITION

# CHAPTER 1

# HUMAN EVOLUTION

*The saddest aspect of life right now is that science gathers knowledge faster than society gathers wisdom.*
— Isaac Asimov

IN THIS SECTION WE TAKE a closer look at the human condition. If you do not yet have a good and compelling reason to change and grow, maybe here you will find one. You need to be part of the solution, not part of the problem.

Albert Einstein said it like this: "It has become appallingly obvious that our technology has exceeded our humanity." Einstein died on April 18, 1955, before the advent of color television, laptop computers, tablets, satellites, cable and satellite television, cell phones, robotics, drones, and so much more. Could you even imagine the early technologies of his time that he was referring to? Though, with the destruction of Hiroshima and Nagasaki, Japan, in 1945, he could have been referring to the rushing in of the nuclear age.

Have we reached a new high in human-developed technology? Have we reached the point where our technological capabilities have surpassed our ability to effectively control ourselves and their use?

The funny thing about what we believe in — sometimes it has nothing to do with the real world. Beliefs may only represent the limits of our current knowledge base. For example, ancient people believed that the world was composed of the four basic elements (wind, earth, fire, and water) and that the world was flat and that Earth was at the center of the universe. More recently, we all grew up believing that Pluto (discovered in 1930) was the ninth and farthest planet in our solar system; until 2006, when Pluto was declared to be only a dwarf planet. We now know for sure the Earth is not flat and that it is not at the center of the universe (Nicolaus Copernicus changed those beliefs in 1514). Today we believe in 117 atomic elements (the list has slowly grown) and that each of those elements is composed of subatomic particles: electrons, protons, and neutrons, which comprise quarks, leptons, neutrinos, muons, bosons, and others — or so we currently believe. New information can change our beliefs.

Our current collective belief is that science holds all the answers to solve life's problems. In turn, we have turned scientific beliefs into a religion, complete with its own prophets (such as Stephen Hawking and Carl Sagan), its own cosmology, and its own sins and penances. This belief in secular science challenges our old beliefs in a more spiritual world. These two presumably opposing belief systems — science and spirituality — vie for us to trust that what they each provide is the "truth" and all the right answers.

But one mystery science has not yet resolved is that of human purpose[9]: why are we here and what are we supposed to do here? Science provides us a better understanding of how our world works, but that still leaves us with questions of how to use that information and for what purpose.

## Change in Technology

Let us examine whether we are any better off today than, let's say, a hundred or thousand years ago. Let us look at where our technology has brought us. Here is a quick look at the history, evolution, and development of key human technologies:

---

9 Purpose — the objective or point of our existence (at work, in relationships, and in life in general).

**War and conflict resolution.** It all started tens of thousands of years ago with sticks and stones, and when that proved to be insufficient, we then moved on to clubs, axes, and swords. And then close-combat fighting gave way to more long-distance fighting using spears, bows and arrows, and, eventually, the catapult and trebuchet.

Then the invention of gunpowder led to the development of guns and cannons. Eventually, fighting on land was too limiting and so we moved combat to the water, with battleships and submarines, and to the air, with airplanes and jet fighters.

With the advent of explosive materials like TNT, we created bombs, and rockets and missiles to deliver those bombs. But the bomb of all bombs is the nuclear bomb. On July 16, 1945, we finally unleashed the most energetic and destructive force in nature, the atom. Along the way we have also created tanks, laser weapons, and unmanned aerial vehicles (UAV). Soon we will have robots fighting our wars; it cannot get more disconnected than that.

Each technological improvement we have created in waging war has been followed by an equally incremental improvement in our defense capability: castles were strongholds against clubs and swords but were made obsolete by catapults and trebuchets. Shields, chainmail armor, and radar have undergone the same obsolescence. Our abilities to defend against and kill each other are locked in an endless horserace.

**Communications.** The ability to exchange thoughts, ideas, emotions, and information distinguishes humans from most animals. Our ability to communicate has certainly come a long way from the early days of shouts, drums, horns, smoke signals, runners, and the Pony Express.

After the discovery of electricity, our ability to communicate figuratively exploded, starting with use of the telegraph in the mid-1800s, followed by the hard-wired telephone. The discovery of radio waves led to walkie-talkies, radios, television, satellites, and cellular telephones. Today, in addition to just talking, we can email, text, and tweet.

We have most certainly improved the distance, speed, and quantity but, sadly, not the quality of our communications. A lot of times, we miss the opportunity to say the right things — to make a positive difference in someone's life.

**Transportation.** When life on this planet first evolved, we crawled out of the goo. And then we learned to walk and run. When that seemed too slow or too hard, we tamed the horse, the camel, the elephant, and the ox to aid us in our work and travels.

Once we discovered and perfected the wheel, well, nothing could stop us, with the cart, the wagon, the bicycle, the motorcycle, the automobile, and the train. To travel on water, we created boats and ships of all sizes and shapes, from ones driven by wind to ones driven by motors, from ones that float to submarines that glide under the water's surface.

When traveling on the surface of our planet was no longer good enough, we duplicated the birds and created airplanes, jets, and spacecraft. I know many people who will not be happy with any form of transportation until someone invents the *Star Trek* transporter — "Beam me up, Scotty."

**Energy.** After food, clothing, and shelter, discovering sources and generating energy have been some of humanity's greatest technological achievements. First, we rubbed two sticks together to make fire and harnessed draft animals to do work.

We then learned how to harness the wind and water and created windmills and waterwheels; later we dammed the rivers to generate hydroelectric power. Today we can capture the energy of the sun with a variety of solar collection methods; we harness the energy in ocean waves, petroleum, and coal and use chemical and nuclear energy to run power plants, our homes, and automobiles. We are still thinking up better and safer ways to produce more energy.

Our prosperity has led to the largest consumption of electrical and petroleum-based power ever. There is no end to the amount of energy consumption and we are still only a "light switch away" from being tossed back into the dark ages. Ask anyone who has ever had to survive the days and weeks in the aftermath of a tornado, hurricane, flood, earthquake, or any other natural or man-made disaster.

**Medicine.** Our basic survival needs motivate us to recover from sickness or injury as quickly as possible. Early on, care of sick and injured people was more of an art than science, from rubbing leaves on bodies to administering potions. In some cultures, healing was more spiritual than scientific. Some illnesses were considered the work of demons and devils, and cures were based on some form of eradication, like getting rid of a pest. Cures and medicines were all sourced from the natural world, and many individuals came along to fill the role of healer: witch doctors, shamans, snake oil salesmen, and eventually nurses and doctors.

We eventually discovered the connection between our environment and our health and that our health is affected by biological objects (such as germs, viruses, and bacteria) invading our body, relieving us of the belief that our health was subject to the whims of omnipotent gods or demons. Today we struggle with a conflict between belief in the efficacy of Eastern and Western medicine. In Western civilization, we dismissed the holistic, spiritual aspect of health care and put faith in scientific resolution of symptoms through surgery and pharmaceuticals. Modern science may soon give us the ability to modify our genes and DNA, potentially relieving us of sicknesses and illnesses before they happen.

Hundreds of health studies point to diet and exercise as the top factors in influencing our health and well-being, followed by genetics and risk-taking behavior. We hardly ever consider that some illnesses may start in our heads and then work its way into our bodies.

Modern medicine promises to extend the human life span to 120 years; the advent of bionics and body-part replacements heralds the possibility of extending life almost indefinitely. All this modern medicine is driven by the promise of a better quality of life. Or is it driven by the fear of death in a more materialistic than spiritual world?

## Growth in Humanity

With all these technological advancements, is there any doubt that human capability to produce new technology is endless? So it is clear, human beings can effect change in our environment, and we have. For tens of thousands of years, we have made these advances for the purpose of making our lives better, easier, safer, and enriched in one way or another. And for this, we should be very proud of our species.

But a follow-on question is — how much have human beings ourselves really improved, changed, or evolved? Not the circumstances of our life, but our humanity? To get a sense of how little the human condition has progressed in more than twenty-five hundred years, listen to the comments of some of the greatest ancient philosophers regarding their times:

- "We hang the petty thieves and appoint the great ones to public office." Aesop, Greek slave and fable author (620 — 560 BC)
- "He that is discontented in one place will seldom be happy in another." Aesop
- "When there is an income tax, the just man will pay more and the unjust less on the same amount of income." Plato, ancient Greek philosopher (427–347 BC)
- "If liberty and equality, as is thought by some, are chiefly to be found in democracy, they will be best attained when all persons alike share in government to the utmost." Aristotle, ancient Greek philosopher (384–322 BC)
- "The young are permanently in a state resembling intoxication." Aristotle
- "By all means, marry. If you get a good wife, you'll become happy; if you get a bad one, you'll become a philosopher." Socrates, ancient Greek philosopher (469–399 BC)
- "The secret of change is to focus all of your energy not on fighting the old but on building the new." Socrates

- "The object of life is not to be on the side of the majority, but to escape finding oneself in the ranks of the insane." Marcus Aurelius, Roman soldier (AD 121–180)

It appears that our human nature has not evolved much in the last two thousand years. Really, the only thing better in our lives today is that we have pretty much handled our survival needs — food, shelter, and clothing issues. Because we have secured our basic survival needs we have now moved on to entertaining ourselves.

We entertain ourselves now more than ever. Cable TV has more than two hundred channels, running twenty-four hours a day, seven days a week. Happy hour in bars and restaurants now runs for hours. Working and earning a living has become a bother — it gets in the way of our entertainment and our lifestyle of acquiring and having things. Earning a living (or providing for our family) is no longer life's purpose or struggle; we have moved beyond that on to entertainment. It is clear that all these material changes and improvements have done little to improve our humanity, the quality of our relationships, or the depth of our spiritual lives and connection to the greater universe.

Let's look at different areas of our lives to see whether our humanity has grown:

**Religion and spirituality.** Many people's spiritual lives are generally defined by the organized religion they associate with, how often they attend religious services, and how well they adhere to their belief system. Most interesting is that spirituality and religion have been a part of the human experience for tens of thousands of years. Early religions recognized a pantheon of major and minor gods. Then somewhere around three thousand to four thousand years ago, the concept of monotheism came on the scene. Today the top three monotheistic religions are Christianity, Islam, and Judaism, with Hinduism and Buddhism rounding out the top five worldwide religions, including another twenty or so organized religions.

Having in our lives a religious (or spiritual) connection to a greater power is significant. It adds perceived benefits to our character. What is most significant about religion is its purpose in the human experience. Not all religions share the same purpose, but in general most religions are belief systems that try to:

- explain things about the universe that we do not understand,
- have us adhere to certain moral and ethical conduct,
- define a structure and lifestyle for us to live within,
- create and define a purpose for our existence, and
- help us develop a relationship with God, some other deity, or a life force.

Religion gives us something bigger than ourselves to be accountable to, something that creates a structure for our lives and sets standards to live by. Religion evolved in an attempt to address the part of our humanity that science and technological advances could not — how and why we are different from the animals.

Unfortunately, human beings have corrupted religion over many thousands of years with our human-nature issues. We have used it as a banner to wage wars, to enslave people, to judge other people's beliefs, and to control the lives of those who do not understand the uniqueness of their spiritual capacity. With our belief in modern technology and because people resist the dogma of most organized religions, today large numbers of people are either leaving religion or associating with a diluted version of one they may have grown up with.

**Conflict and war.** Ever since Cain attacked his brother, Abel, and killed him, human beings have been engaging in conflicts with each other. Driven by numerous factors of human nature, we have found so many reasons to be mad at or upset with one another:

- Ideologies
- Resources and economics
- Show-of-force and control

Often these reasons masquerade as other excuses, but generally these all come down to one reason: a human-nature-driven power struggle. Sometimes conflicts escalate to full-fledged battles and wars, with warring parties battling it out in the courtroom, in the streets, or on the battlefield. No matter how much human beings talk of peace, we constantly battle with each other.

Our human nature constantly struggles with this dichotomy — peace and war. Within the last 260 years we have not gone more than a single twenty-five-year period (one human generation) without a major war or conflict somewhere in the world:

- 1755 to 1763 Seven Years War (French and Indian War)
- 1775 to 1783 American Revolutionary War
- 1792 to 1802 French Revolutionary Wars
- 1803 to 1815 Napoleonic Wars
- 1812 to 1815 War of 1812
- 1830 European Revolutions
- 1846 to 1848 Mexican-American War
- 1850 to 1864 Taiping Rebellion (Taiping Civil War)
- 1854 to 1856 Crimean War
- 1861 to 1865 American Civil War
- 1870 to 1871 Franco-Prussian War
- 1898 to 1898 Spanish-American War
- 1899 to 1901 Boxer Rebellion
- 1904 to 1905 Russo-Japanese War
- 1910 to 1920 Mexican Revolution
- 1912 to 1913 Balkan Wars
- 1914 to 1918 World War I
- 1917 to 1922 Russian Civil War
- 1936 to 1939 Spanish Civil War
- 1939 to 1940 Soviet-Finnish War
- 1939 to 1945 World War II*
- 1946 to 1991 Cold War
- 1948 to 2006 Arab-Israeli Wars
- 1950 to 1953 Korean War
- 1959 to 1975 Vietnam War
- 1967 to 1970 Biafran War (Nigerian Civil War)
- 1980 to 1988 Iran-Iraq War
- 1982 Falklands War

- 1990 to 1991 (First) Gulf War
- 1996 to 2003 Congo Wars
- 2001 to present War in Afghanistan
- 2003 to 2010 Iraq War (Second Gulf War)

* The deadliest war in human history, WWII brought about an estimated 60–85 million fatalities.

> *"In the last 3000 years there has only been around 250 recorded years of peace, with no international wars."*
> *—www.listzblog.com*

Had enough?

Somehow our human nature drives us to conflict and war. We do not want it, but we just cannot seem to figure out how to avoid it. Clearly, modern human beings have made no progress in this arena.

**Relationships and marriage.** We also wage war — though sometimes not as dramatically as global conflict — in our personal relationships. So many of our relationships are in trouble; spouses do not get along with each other, children with their parents, siblings with siblings, neighbors with neighbors. Friends, family, and spouses — these are some of our most significant and important relationships, as are our relationships with business associates, coworkers, bosses, club members, and acquaintances. If relationships are so important, then why are we so bad at maintaining successful relationships? [10]

The degree to which human beings engage in relationships and the quality of those relationships are key indicators of how well we are actually getting along, successfully interacting with each other, and making a difference in each other's lives. Marriage is one of the most important types of relationship. Its positive and negative effects are felt by the many individuals in the family group. Marital

---

10 Successful relationship — In a successful relationship, the needs of the relationship are prioritized before the needs of the individuals. It demonstrates the ability of two people to get along, communicate, and compromise to meet the needs of the relationship. In a successful marriage, the happy and loving couple stays together for the life.

relationships can be used as a key indicator of our overall relationship abilities.

We know not all marriages are successful. Many end in divorce (and some should have ended sooner than they did). Therefore, divorce could be one way to measure just how well couples communicate, interact with each other, and work out life's issues together. According to online legal services company Avvo, the chances of first marriages in the United States ending in separation or divorce is close to 50 percent:

> *"Ah, yes, divorce, from the Latin word meaning to rip out a man's genitals through his wallet."*
> Robin Williams

- 20 percent within 5 years
- 32 percent within 10 years
- 40 percent within 15 years
- 48 percent within 20 years

Second marriages have a much lower rate of success:

- 10 percent within 1 year
- 31 percent within 5 years
- 46 percent within 10 years

With these kinds of statistics, it is not hard to see how little our humanity — of which communication and relationships are fundamental components — has changed.

Couples have many reasons for getting married and many more for failures of relationships. More times than not, our disagreements with relationship partners come down to a handful of issues:

- Who is right and who is wrong
- Winning the argument (instead of seeing both sides of the argument)
- Controlling the situation (versus empowering people)
- Believing that I am better than you, and making a point of it

As with global conflict, our failed personal relationships can be traced to one deep-seated cause: a human-nature-driven power struggle between parties. The weapons may vary from time to time and couple to couple, but the results are usually the same — destroyed relationships, children torn between parents, friends needing to pick sides, and so on.

Global conflicts are reflections of our relationships at home. We cannot expect the world to behave any better or any different from how we do in our relationships. We may not have one standard for ourselves and a separate (more restrictive, demanding) standard for others. If we want peace in the world, then we must start by creating success and making peace in our own relationships.

## Human Status Quo

Humanity has evolved in our capability to make things smaller, better, faster, and deadlier, but we still have a lot of opportunity to grow in how we deal with each other. We run around under the pretense that human beings have evolved into a "better" species. True, we are not primitive cave-dwellers anymore. The only thing that has significantly changed (over the last two thousand plus years) is our general level of prosperity and a lessening of our struggle to survive.

Only our prosperity hides us from the "evils" of humankind's potential for inhumanity. The capacity to be cruel and inhumane lives within all of us — it is part of our human nature. Only our choices separate us from the animal and the primitive within. Only our level of prosperity keeps us somewhat protected, immune to the daily struggle to survive and competition for resources that bring security.

When will we attend to the other area of human existence — our interrelationship with other human beings? Hunger still exists, war still exists, people still hate their neighbors, and family members still do not talk to each other. Human beings have been falling behind the evolution curve when it comes to growth in our level of humanity; the Humanity Curve is a flat line, as demonstrated by the greatest acts of inhumanity we have committed — the Holocaust, the Armenian genocide, Darfur, and every human conflict since Cain and Abel's, and every war fought in the name of one god or another.

By no means is this an attempt to belittle human achievement and success. We most certainly live in better times than in years past; people are living longer, more productive lives, with access to more comforts than ever before. But are we any better off as a people — emotionally, spiritually? Have we stopped hating, killing, and making war? Have we accomplished the basic acts of humanity of understanding and loving everyone equally? It is time to now understand our human nature.

> *"Science investigates; religion interprets. Science gives man knowledge which is power; religion gives man wisdom which is control."*
> Martin Luther King, Jr.

## *Key Takeaways*

1. Though humanity has created major achievements in technology, we have not evolved equally from a relational or spiritual perspective.
2. We need to understand ourselves, our human nature, before we can create change in our humanity that moves us forward in how we treat each other and achieve our purpose in life.
3. We need to be part of the solution, not part of the problem.

# CHAPTER 2

# MAN OR ANIMAL

*At his best, man is the noblest of all animals; separated from law and justice he is the worst.*
— Aristotle

It is believed that all living things contain a common life force that defines our existence, identity, and capabilities. Because we are similarly animated by the life force, in many ways we share a lot of common characteristics with all other living beings. Yet certain characteristics set us apart from the animals. Let's see which:

**Intelligence.** We classify people's level of intelligence by their IQ, or intelligence quotient. The top of the IQ scale is 200. IQ of the human population varies; with most people falling in the average range around 100 (see Figure 2):

- Marilyn vos Savant 228
- Leonardo da Vinci 220
- Johann Wolfgang Goethe 210
- Sir Isaac Newton 190
- Bobby Fischer 187
- Galileo 185
- Marilyn Monroe 168
- Thomas Jefferson 160
- Copernicus 160

- Albert Einstein 160
- Bill Gates 160
- Eli Manning 156
- Sharon Stone 154
- Ben Stein 150
- Thomas Edison 145
- Richard Nixon 143
- Adolf Hitler 141
- Natalie Portman 140
- Shakira 140
- Bill Clinton 137
- Arnold Schwarzenegger 135
- Al Gore 134
- John F. Kennedy 119
- George Washington 118
- Al Franken 110
- Ben Roethlisberger 110
- Paris Hilton 107
- Ronald Reagan 105
- Brett Favre 104
- Howard Stern 99
- Dan Marino 92
- OJ Simpson 89
- Andy Warhol 86
- Muhammad Ali 78

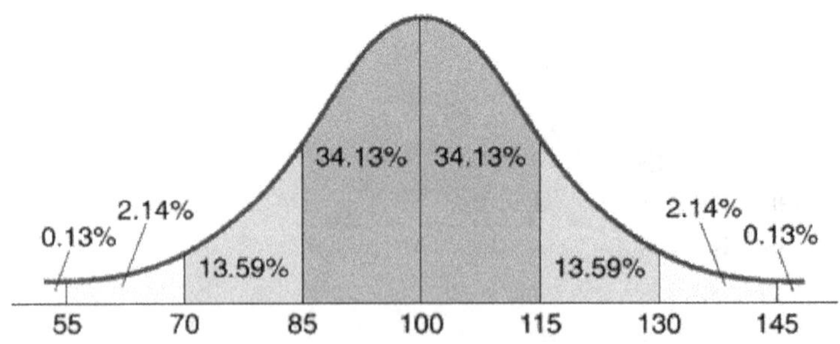


**Figure 2. Scores on a standardized IQ test.**
*Half the population is below average and the other half is above average.*

Though there is no similar IQ charting for animals, I am sure varying levels of intelligence also exist within the animal kingdom. Some animals (various birds, dogs, apes, dolphins, and sea lions) have demonstrated high levels of intelligence, according to human standards. And the lower-intelligent ones probably just do not make it; they get eaten. So, intelligence alone is probably not a characteristic that separates human beings from animals.

**Socializing.** Living alone, living in groups, getting along with others — these are socializing characteristics. Whether prey or predator, animals come in two types, those who live alone and those who live in groups (herds, packs, flocks). Sometimes when animals live in groups, these groups have a structure or organization, with a leader or an alpha male or female or some sort of social hierarchy.

Human beings seem to socialize in similar patterns. Some people are loners; we call them hermits, and they live as far as possible from society and want nothing to do with other people. Most people live, play, and work together in family groups, clubs, communities, towns, and cities. Some groups of human beings take on characteristics similar to that of predatory pack animals; we call them gangs. So, socializing is probably not a characteristic that separates human beings from animals.

**Survival.** Survival is about obtaining enough food and water, keeping safe, and reproducing. No living organism can exist for more than a generation without handling its survival needs. Here again, animals and human beings share many characteristics, except humans are at the top of all the food chains.

In the beginning, we were all hunter-gatherers. We ate what was on the ground or in the trees, or we hunted animals for food and clothing. Today most people do not need to hunt or gather, except maybe to collect the bargains at their neighborhood grocery store. Almost all the meat and vegetables we eat today are farmed, packaged, and available at stores for our convenience; we no longer need to get our hands bloody or dirty.

However, all undomesticated animals are hunter-gatherers of one variety or another. Their survival still depends on their ability to find or kill the food they need to live. And when one animal kills another animal, this is not murder but survival of the fittest, the law of nature, the circle of life, eat or be eaten.

When it comes to safety, animals have two motivations: protect themselves and the group from being eaten, and safeguard their territory so that they have enough resources to survive. One animal group does not go to war against another group for any other purpose. Once a pack of lions takes down a gazelle for dinner, the entire Serengeti community returns to what it was doing, usually coexisting around the waterhole. With most animals, one or both parents safeguard the young. Some animals protect their young in a communal environment. One animal will kill another animal for one of only three reasons: defense and security, food, or dominance.

In regard to safety, human beings are similar to animals. Human parents also go to great lengths to protect their young. In general, human beings will kill another animal or another human being for one of those same three reasons: defense and security, food, or dominance.[11] However, in the case of human beings, disputes over dominance can pit one person against another or one group, such as families, communities, or countries, against another. Survival instinct is most certainly a common characteristic shared by animals and human beings, so it does not separate us from the animals, though our day-to-day practice of survival differs from theirs.

**Creativity and adaptability.** Human beings have a lot in common with other animals when it comes to intelligence, socializing, and survival. Yet we are imbued with something unique that makes us different

> *"It is not the strongest of the species that survives, nor the most intelligent that survives. It is the one that is most adaptable to change."*
> Charles Darwin

---

11 Dominance — to gain territory, control, and leadership or, in some cases, to prove a point of who is "right."

from all the other animals: creativity. Our ability to adapt, a form of creativity, goes beyond mere evolutionary adaptation. With limited creativity, animals that cannot adapt or change in time go extinct. The unique quality of human beings is our innate ability to change and adapt to our environment or to adapt our environment to us. Our creative abilities alter our environment to meet our needs and fulfill our desires.

Part of our adaptability is our mobility. We have moved from one place to another, migrating from land to land and continent to continent. Early human beings migrated thousands of miles from Africa and Asia to all over the world, motivated by food, famine, climate, or want of a better view. We progressed from hunter-gatherers to farmers to herders. We went from living in trees and caves to using wood, stone, and earth to build shelter wherever we went. Creativity and adaptability are significant characteristics that separate human beings from animals.

## Key Takeaways

1. Animals and human beings share many characteristics: intelligence, socializing, survival.
2. Human beings are unique in that we create, adapt, and alter our environment to fit our needs beyond our need to survive, even as the environment around us changes.

# CHAPTER 3

# HUMAN NATURE: EXCUSE OR JUSTIFICATION?

*Everyone makes mistakes in life, but that does not mean they have to
pay for them the rest of their life. Sometimes good people make bad
choices. It does not mean they are bad... It means they are human.*
— Anonymous

ALL HUMAN BEINGS HAVE IN common our human nature. It is what
drives us. It is the way we behave, interact, and respond to the events
and people around us in each and every moment of our lives. Human
nature is in effect at all times. It is not something we can turn off
at our choosing. And it is most certainly not our personality, for
that is an individual characteristic. Human nature is our collective
human characteristics and descriptive of the entire human species. It
is wired in every human being, regardless of sex, sexual preference,
race, ethnicity, or even who your parents are. It is even more than
our DNA because DNA represents only our physical entity. Human
nature animates our entire being.

How many times have you heard someone admit, "Mistakes
happen. No one is perfect. I'm only human!" or some version thereof?
Probably more than a few times. How often have you used the same

expression — "Mistakes happen. I'm only human!" Probably more than a few times. When we use these expressions, it is usually in our own defense for an act that did not go as planned and we mean to justify the imperfection or diminish its impact.

We are relieved, of course, that our humanity allows us some degree of failure and that failure is somehow acceptable because of our humanity. Because it is not all our fault, because our humanness gets in the way, we can evade taking total responsibility for errors, omissions, or bad results. We most certainly feel better when everyone uses the same escape plan — "I'm only human!" — and gets away with it. The best part; the more other people use this excuse and get away with it, the easier it is for everybody to use it.

On the other hand, how did you feel when someone used those same words and that expression? Did you give them a free pass for their transgression because of their human failing? Or did you find the "I'm only human!" expression a useless cop-out, a convenient and lame excuse that demonstrates the person's lack of responsibility?

Where do we draw the line between justification and cop-out? Or is one really just the same as the other? Is human nature a blessing or a curse? A blessing, because we can use it as a standing justification for our lack of perfection; a curse, because no matter how hard we try, we can never obtain perfection. Let's discover which it is.

Human beings seem to be set up with an opposing set of priorities. Motivations and behaviors that run contrary to each other war within us:

- Laziness versus productivity
- Emotion versus logic
- Selfishness versus selflessness
- Arrogance versus humility
- Faith versus free will
- Chance versus predictability
- Greediness versus generosity
- Grudges versus forgiveness
- Fear versus confidence

Classic depictions of human nature show a little white angel and a little red devil sitting on our shoulders, whispering in our ears, telling us what to do (see Figure 3). Here is our problem: we have to choose wisely which one to listen to, but how?

**Figure 3. Whom do I listen to, the angel or the devil?**

If human nature consists of all those things in the list above, and more, did we get dealt a royal flush or a garbage hand? Some people say that we were set up to fail; how else can we understand having these conflicting drives at the core of our being?

In reality, we were not set up to fail but to be challenged — challenged to be conscious of how our thoughts guide our actions and words, challenged not to do things automatically or take every word and action for granted. And these challenges set us apart from the other animals. Does the lion wake up in the morning and ponder "How am I going to be a better lion today?"

As we will discover and explore further throughout the book, there are many "problems and challenges" embedded within our human nature. The *problem* is our human nature presents us with two ways of being (as listed above). The *challenge* is two-fold: first, recognizing and knowing we *have* options and second, being able, knowledgeable, and flexible to *choose* the proper path to take. The proper choosing depends on the many in-the-moment conditions and circumstances of the situation; there is no one right answer. The book will present the circumstances, the options, and the pluses and minuses of each problem, but we are still left with the choosing, and this depends on the long-term results we want to achieve.

Here is what being human is like; imagine you are a rollercoaster car chugging up that first long and tall climb to the top. What is at the top? What most people call happiness, success, and a meaningful life, for you and the people you also carry along in the rollercoaster car. Making "right" decisions is the chain pulling you up. Each time you fail, you slip back a notch or two, depending on the scope of the failure. To make it to the top in a smooth and fast ascent, you need to keep making the "right" decisions; otherwise, it becomes a very bumpy, stressful, protracted ride to the top, if ever you make it.

## Exercise Break

Make a list of human-nature issues you struggle with and under which specific circumstances. Here are a few examples:

- There is a person at work and she is always arguing with me about everything. I can never win.
- I am always being taken advantage of in my relationships; I can't find love.
- Whenever I get upset about something that happens at home, I need to go shopping or I'm eating a bowl of ice cream.
- I hate talking with my mother. She's always making me feel guilty about everything I do in my life.
- Every day is an emotional rollercoaster ride; happy one minute and a minute later I am in tears. I can't control it.

## *Key Takeaways*

1. Human nature is what determines our everyday responses to the events and interactions of the world.
2. Human nature is not something we can turn off at our choosing.
3. Human nature is something we need to learn to control and interact with, not ignore, and certainly not try to run away from.
4. Human beings were set up with a challenge — to be better than the animals; therefore, we need to choose at each moment which path to take and which decision to make and then be responsible for the consequences of those actions and choices.

SECTION 2

# INTERNAL HUMAN OPERATING SYSTEM REVEALED

# CHAPTER 4

# HUMAN COMPOSITION

*Modern philosophy has never been able quite to shake off the
Cartesian idea of mind, as something that "resides"... Everybody
laughs at this nowadays, and yet everybody continues to think of mind
in this same general way, as something within this person or that,
belonging to him and correlative to the real world. A whole course of
lectures would be required to expose this error.*
— Charles Sanders Peirce, American philosopher

AT THIS POINT, I HOPE you have discovered or developed a good and
compelling reason to learn more about our human nature. Here, we
begin the process of understanding the fundamentals of the human
being by applying reverse engineering.

Various cultures and religious practices describe human beings
as consisting of three basic parts — the mind, body, and soul (or
spirit). Let's start with this generally accepted model of the human
being and explore its details. From here we are going to dive into
the form and nature of human beings and develop a functional
understanding that describes how we work. Upon that, we will build
an overall operational model[12] of the human being with all its parts;

---

12 Operational model — a representation of a real-world phenomenon for the purpose of
understanding, communicating, and conveying its fundamental principles and functionality.

this model is called the Human Control System (HCS). At its center is the internal Human Operating System (iHOS) (see Figure 4).

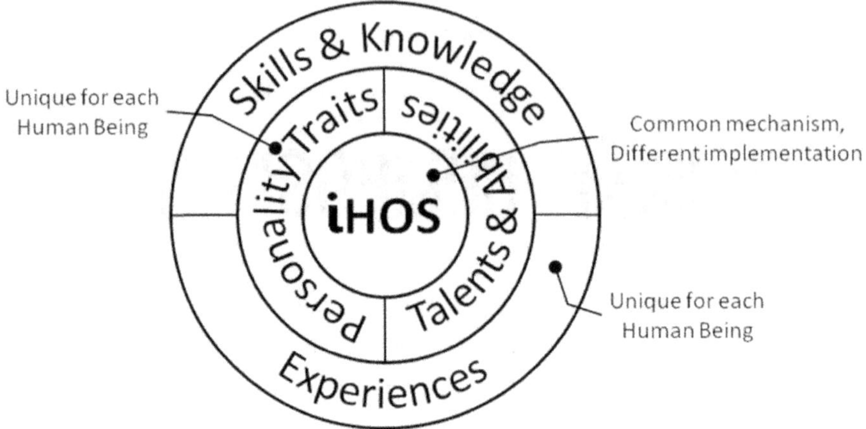


**Figure 4. Our iHOS is at the heart of who we are.**
*The iHOS is the same for all of us; all other characteristics are unique for each human being.*

What makes each of us unique is, first, what we are born with: our talents, abilities, and personality traits; and, second, the characteristics we accumulate along the path of life: our skills, knowledge, and experiences. But our internal Human Operating System is common to all. It determines and drives our passions, motivations, and accomplishments. Understanding our internal Human Operating System is key to understanding ourselves and others and key to change and growth. We begin with exploring the body.

## The Body

The body interacts and interfaces directly with the realities of life, like driving a car, drinking coffee, working out, working, and with other human beings. The body is made up of several physical subsystems, such as a skeleton, muscles, circulatory system, nervous system, and many organs.

The skeleton gives shape and form to the body. The muscles give the skeleton the ability to articulate, move, and interact with objects around it. The organs perform vital bodily functions: vision, hearing, breathing, digestion, immunity, and reproduction. Our ability to control these bodily functions appears to be both voluntary (conscious) and involuntary (unconscious) (see Table 1).

## Table 1. Control of Human Bodily Functions

| Bodily Function | Degree of Control | |
|---|---|---|
| | Voluntary | Involuntary |
| Vision | Eye motion | Focus, converting to recognizable images |
| Hearing | Putting your hands over your ears | Converting to recognizable sounds |
| Breathing | Breathing rate, holding breath | Holding breath too long, passing out, starting to breathe again |
| Digestion | What you put in your mouth | Converting food to energy and nutrition |
| Immunity | Getting your vaccinations, vitamins, supplements | Fighting infections and injuries |
| Reproduction | Sex with whom and when, contraception, having an abortion | Monthly cycles, fertilization, having a baby |

Involuntary bodily functions are performed without conscious thought, meaning they occur whether we think about them or not. Even walking, after we develop the skill as children, does not require much conscious thought. We just put one foot in front of the other, and off we go. Same for thinking — thoughts just seem to pop into our head without any active consideration. It seems like our involuntary bodily functions are controlled by something, just not our conscious self.

Our voluntary bodily functions seem easier to understand because they are under "our" control. But voluntary bodily functions are performed at a high level of awareness beneath which many involuntary functions are at work.

Now, if we compare the human being to a computer or robotic system, then the body is analogous to the computer's hardware,[13] the physical components of the computing system. Not a perfect analogy, though, because human beings are much more complex than computers or of any of today's robots.

The human body has parts that perform functions similar to a computer's hardware: the skin is analogous to the case in which all the other hardware is contained and it, along with the skeleton, gives shape and form to the body. The brain is where logic and information processing take place, like a computer's central processing unit (CPU); it also stores data as a computer's memory does. The spine and nervous system are analogous to the backplane or motherboard of the computer, where all internal communications between input and output devices occur. The input and output systems of the computer, the display, keyboard, and mouse, for example, transfer data in and out of the computer, similar to the body's input and output devices:

- Senses (inputs) — sight, sound, taste, touch, smell, and motion
- Limbs (outputs) — arms/hands/fingers and legs/feet/toes
- Mouth (output) — sounds and speech

Like the computer, the body receives data. It processes the data into information, stores it for future reference and access, and creates some form of output, either verbal communication or action.

Also, as computers have different power-down modes (i.e., sleep and hibernate), human beings have different levels of activity and inactivity:

- Active mode
- Idle mode
- Sleep mode
- Even a "chill" mode

But, unlike a computer, a human being cannot be turned off; that would be fatal. A human being runs 24/7. A human being also does

---

13 Computer hardware — this includes the case, display, keyboard, mouse, hard drive, and all the electronics inside the case.

not have battery backup to save the contents of its memory should the power be interrupted, nor does it have a master reset button (Ctrl+Alt+Del) to restart it in "safe mode" when things go bad.

The body deals with the ordinary and mundane physical portions of our lives. Fundamentally, our body is not much different from the bodies of other mammals and animals. However, as discussed earlier, it is not our body that sets us apart from the other animals.

## The Soul

As compared to the body, the next component of the human being is more abstract and unseen, and that part is the soul. The soul is the life source that animates the body[14] and drives its voluntary and involuntary functions. The soul gives us a sense of purpose, motivations, goals, and objectives. Some refer to the soul as the *psyche* or the *spirit*. The soul brings life to the body and causes it to think and feel and act out in the environment.

Though some people may not believe in this "spiritual" component or they may not be familiar with it, the concept of the soul supplies the missing component in the understanding of the human condition and our human nature. Unlike the body, the soul is something we cannot touch or even see. Its existence we must take on faith. I suspect there are

> *"We are not human beings having a spiritual experience. We are spiritual beings having a human experience."*
> Pierre Teilhard de Chardin

other things in your life that you take on faith. Just add one more for now. It is an important part of the operational model.[15]

---

14  Body — this is the vessel for the soul to reside in so that it can interact with the "real world."

15  Side note: In 1901, physician Duncan MacDougall attempted to scientifically prove the existence of the immortal human soul. His goal was to record the loss of body weight immediately following death, which would represent the departure of the soul. He performed his experiment on five dying individuals. He reported a weight loss of 21 grams at the death of the first patient. His findings have never been validated.

Fortunately, we can postulate the existence of a soul by the results it produces and by the effects it has on reality. It's like gravity — it is there, but we cannot see it or touch it. We can only measure its effects and then put a name to the results.

Modern medicine has learned much about the human body. Medicine can cure a lot of what ails us, prolonging life in healthier bodies. On the other hand, religions over the millennia have explored and tried to teach us about the human spirit. But we often miss the point of the teachings; we get lost in or are driven away by religious dogma. Most people overlook the purpose of religion, as a system we can use to develop a deeper connection to our self, to understand our purpose and humanity's bigger purpose, and to connect us with the energy of life all around us.

We earlier compared the body to computer hardware. Many refer to the CPU as the "brains" of the computer, and similarly the human body has a brain that is the control point of the body. Computer software is loaded into the CPU, which executes the applications that direct the hardware to do what we intend it to do.

So, the soul is analogous to software; it is "loaded" into the human brain, where it executes bodily functions. The soul operates in the human being in two ways: first, it is connected to the body and controls the body's functions; and, second, it connects us to other souls and the infinite possibilities of the universe.

## The Mind

So far, we have addressed the body and the soul parts of the mind-body-soul trilogy. The mind part is harder to address because it does not exist as a physical component or in a place, as do the body and the soul. Some theories or spiritual practices suggest the mind resides in the brain or that it is the brain, or that our thoughts are our mind.

However, the mind is really the manifestation of the soul connecting to the body. It is the conjunction where body and soul coexist and interact (see Figure 5). The mind is how and where the soul perceives its existence in the body. It is the illusionary place where the soul has "real-world" consciousness. It is the illusionary place where the soul argues or discusses with itself what it wants or what it should or should not do.

> *"Thinking: the talking of the soul with itself."*
> Plato

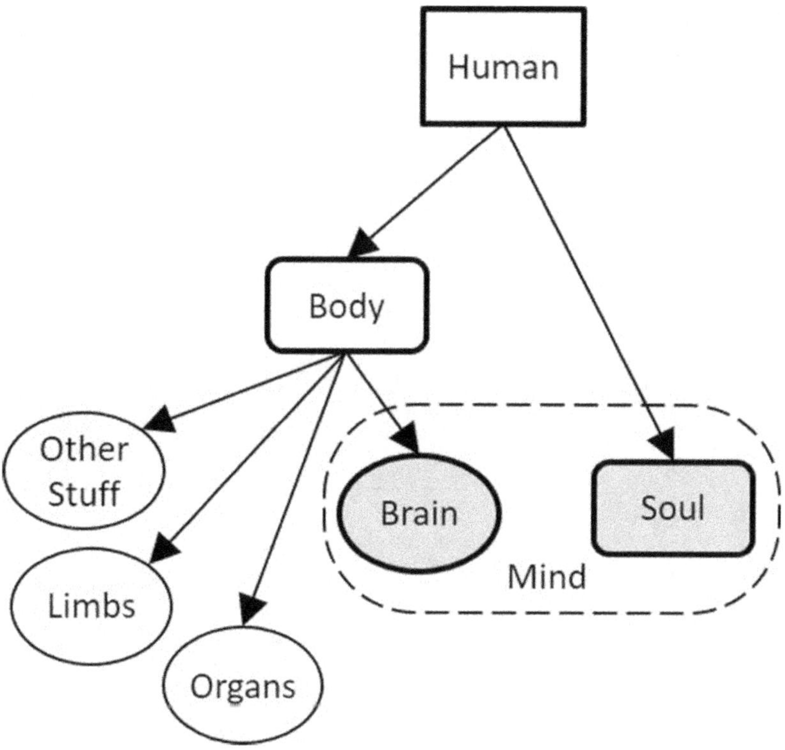


**Figure 5. Composition of the human being.**

So, in computer system terms, the brain is the CPU of the body. The soul is the software that executes its desires via the functionality of the brain, and our perception of that functionality we call the mind. We then associate thought, consciousness, and self-talk (all the chatter that goes on in our head) as being centered in the mind. In our operational model of the human being (the Human Control System) the mind has no real place.

## Key Takeaways

1. When compared to a computer system, the body is similar to computer hardware, and the soul is similar to computer software, and the internal Human Operating System is the soul, the body's software.
2. Mind does not physically exist. The mind is the manifestation of the soul connecting to the body, the conjunction where both body and soul coexist and interact.
3. You *are* your soul; you *have* a body.

# HUMAN CONTROL SYSTEM

*You never change things by fighting the*
*existing reality. To change something, build a new model*
*that makes the existing model obsolete.*
— Buckminster Fuller, visionary American architect

WHEN COMPARING A HUMAN BEING to a robot, we can say that both have certain similarities; both are real-time, computer-driven, stimulus-response control systems. However, the human's control system is certainly much more elaborate and complex than a robot's. Nevertheless, the analogy of a real-time, computer-driven, stimulus-response control system does offer some interesting insights into how this Human Control System (HSC) describes the functionality of the human being and how the software portion — the internal Human Operating System (iHOS) — within the HCS controls the hardware portion — the body — and how all this enables us to interact with the environments around us (see Figure 6).

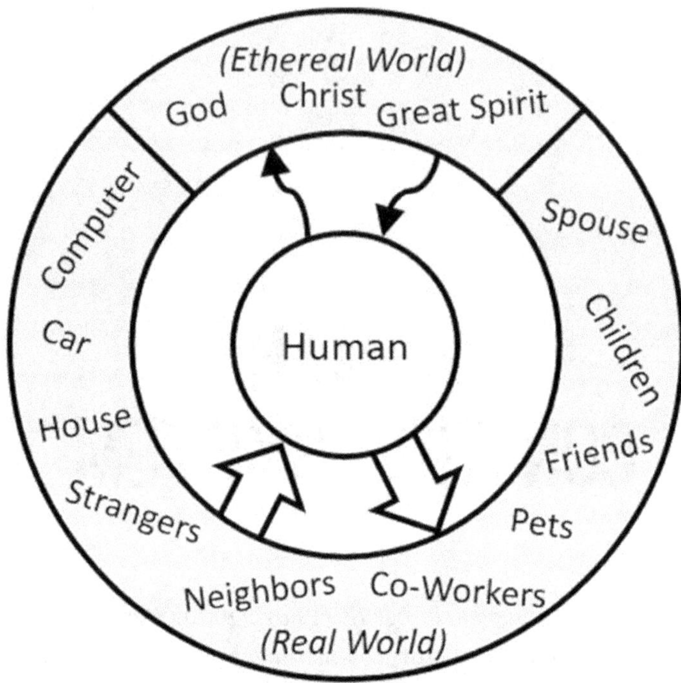


**Figure 6. Human interaction with its environments.**

One environment the human being interacts with is what we refer to as the "real world," consisting of all the inanimate objects (cars, houses, computers, and so on) and all the animate objects (spouses, children, coworkers, friends, strangers, pets, and so on). Another environment is that of the ethereal world, the space where people interact with the universe and a higher power, greater consciousness, or God.

In the HCS, the human being interacts externally with its environments; this is the external control subsystem portion of the HCS. Also part of the HCS are the interactions occurring within the body. The body has its own internal control subsystems — the HCS is a control system within a control system. Within the body there are several distributed control subsystems; such as the energy/feed-me subsystem, the motion/keep-your-balance subsystem, the health-monitoring subsystem, the fight-or-flight subsystem, and many more.

## Operational Model of the Human Control System

The interesting part to know about the Human Control System is how the body and its internal Human Operating System interconnect and interact. In the Human Control System, the body is the hardware that interfaces with the external, real-world environment, using its many senses (input devices) and its arms, legs, and mouth (output devices), and in the internal Human Operating System, the interactive software provides the drive, algorithms, and motivations that run the body. The internal Human Operating System (the soul) filters and processes inputs from the body to produce its output responses: moving or speaking. These two control subsystems (internal and external) together create the Human Control System shown in the operational model in Figure 7.

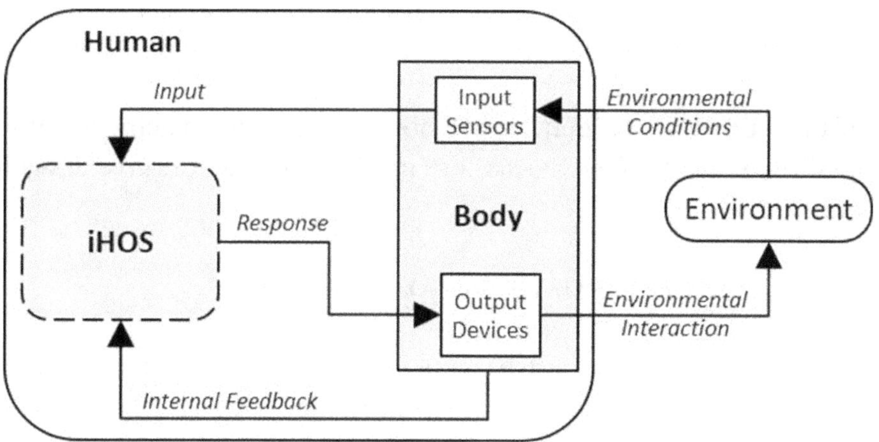


Figure 7. Human Control System operational model.

## Goals and Objectives of the Human Control System

Unlike a robot, a human being is more than a stimulus-response machine that waits around for some change in input to cause an output response. The human being is a combination of a stimulus-response system and an internally motivated being. This internal motivation provides the drive, purpose, and initiative that push us. Human beings self-generate the desired state (the condition we wish to achieve), meaning we create and change our desired states on the basis of internal motivations; we decide to:

- Diet and lose fifteen pounds
- Go back to college and earn a higher degree
- Get married
- Prepare for and run a marathon
- Go to work today
- Be a good spouse today
- Be a good parent today

Within the Human Control System, the soul has influence. It has a set of directives and objectives it drives us to achieve, and these are our motivational factors. Without motivational factors, we would just sit around and do nothing, waiting for the world to do something to us first. Motivational factors drive us in specific directions toward goals or endpoints. When we are born, we set out to achieve these soul directives and objectives; these motivational factors give us each a purpose.

## Boundaries and Limitations

As mentioned previously, the Human Control System has a set of input sensors and output devices. The body receives inputs, and the internal Human Operating System processes them into a related set of output responses for the body to express. Together, the body and soul provide incredible opportunities and possibilities for accomplishing many goals and objectives in life; however, our actual ability to process inputs into outputs does have boundaries and limitations.

These limitations and boundaries are a basic part of the Human Control System operational model. We need to understand our physical and human-derived boundaries and limitations, some of which are universal and others of which are personal; some, mandatory; others, voluntary.

Some limitations are set by the physical laws of nature (gravity, speed of light, etc.). The characteristics of our body establish other physical margins, such as the ability to walk, run, climb, talk, hear, see, or play a sport. The environment imposes another set of physical boundaries, such as time of day, location, and whom you are with (see Table 2).

**Table 2. Human Control System**
**Boundaries and Limitations**

|  | Mandatory | Voluntary |
|---|---|---|
| **Universal** | Gravity<br>Natural laws | Governmental laws<br>Group rules |
| **Personal** | Body capabilities<br>Intellectual capabilities<br>Whom you are with<br>Physical location | Religion<br>Morals<br>Social norms<br>Principles<br>Opinions |

Humankind establishes limitations and boundaries in the form of structured governmental, civil, and organizational rules and laws (too many to enumerate). Religions enact moral and ethical codes, laws, and commandments, and social norms[16] form another set of rules to limit us. Finally, we self-impose some boundaries on ourselves according to what we each believe are possible.

Of course, only the physical laws of nature are truly limiting. All the other various boundaries and limitations are voluntary, assuming you wish to live in peace and quiet with your fellow human beings.

---

16 Social norms — the stories we tell ourselves of what is and is not acceptable within the group.

## *Key Takeaways*

1. The Human Control System is the human being interacting in the environment. The human being is the body (with its input sensors and output devices) driven by the soul.
2. The Human Control System software = internal Human Operating System = the soul.
3. Soul-based motivational factors drive us each in a specific direction to a goal or endpoint.
4. Our body and soul provide incredible opportunities and possibilities in accomplishing many things in life, tempered by physical and human-made boundaries and limitations.

# CHAPTER 6

# INTERNAL HUMAN OPERATING SYSTEM

*It matters not how strait the gate,*
*How charged with punishments the scroll,*
*I am the master of my fate:*
*I am the captain of my soul.*
— W. E. Henley, "Invictus"

IN COMPUTER SOFTWARE TERMS, THE internal Human Operating System is an embedded, multitasking, real-time operating system software package. *Embedded* implies that the operating system is completely contained within the body. *Multitasking* implies that the operating system can handle more than one task at a time. And *real-time* implies that the operating system responds to internal and external events as they happen so that there is no noticeable lag between event and response.

A quick summary of what we know about our internal Human Operating System (iHOS):

- Our soul functions as the internal Human Operating System.
- It manages all our internal bodily functions.

- It brings "life" and animation to our body.
- The body provides the physical means for the internal Human Operating System to interact with other human beings and with the rest of the real world.
- It drives the body to do what it intends to do and determines our response to the world.
- It brings purpose to the physical body.
- It describes how our human nature functions and understanding it provides insight into how and why human beings do what they do and say what they say.

To complete the Human Control System operational model, we must take the concept of the soul and the internal Human Operating System one step deeper, to the advanced level. The key principle of the internal Human Operating System is that the soul comprises two distinct and separate souls that coexist: the Primitive Soul and the Angelic Soul (see Figure 8). They are analogous to the two types of computer software: the manufacturer-installed operating system and the user-installed application programs.

Each of these souls, the Primitive Soul and the Angelic Soul, is distinct, useful, and good. Each has its own set of characteristics and a unique purpose.

From here forward, the "you" to whom I refer is composed of these three parts — your *body*, which contains a *Primitive Soul* and an *Angelic Soul*. This is "you," three united parts, with each serving a distinct and useful purpose in your existence. All three make up who "you" are. No one and nothing can take apart, sell, save, lose, or disconnect these three parts until death; they are all linked to "you."

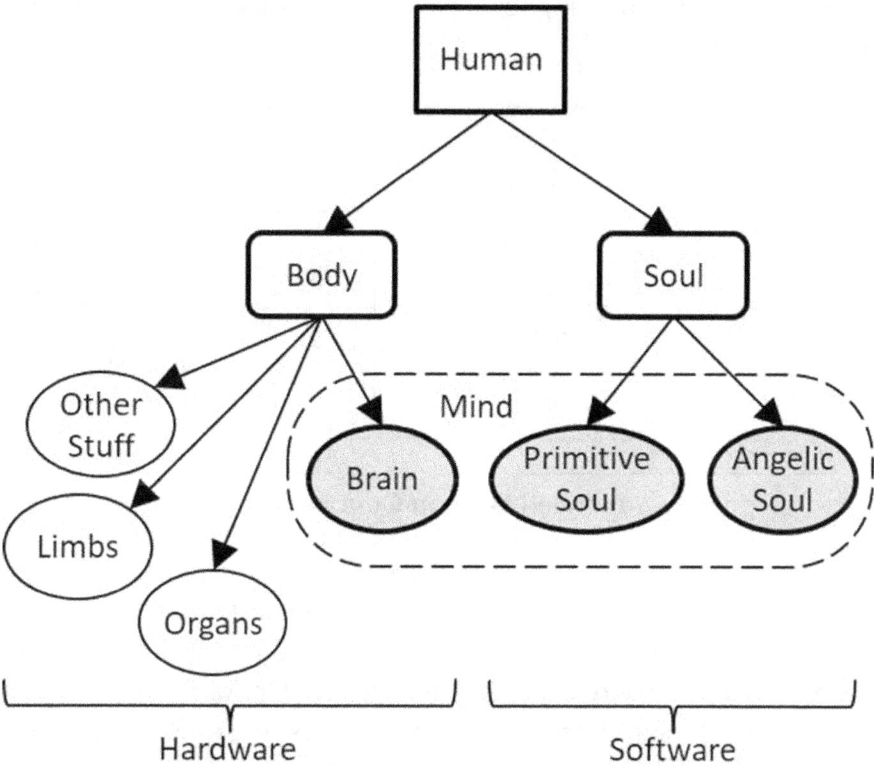


**Figure 8. Composition of the human being —
the advanced version.**

## Upgraded Human Control System Model

The advanced Human Control System operational model shows how the Primitive Soul and Angelic Soul interact within the human being. Because each soul has a unique purpose, each performs different functions within separate control loops. The two control loops are interrelated and cascaded[17] (see Figure 9). The Primitive Soul provides direct internal control of the bodily functions. The

---

17 Cascaded — control loops that are connected in series, one following the other.

Angelic Soul provides higher-order, supervisory control over the Primitive Soul.

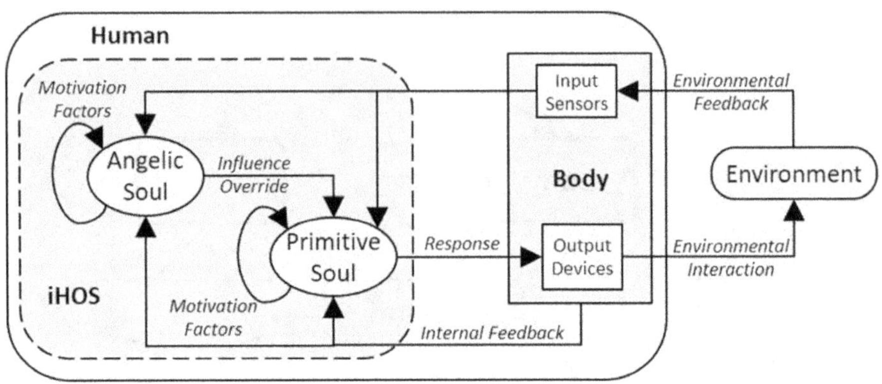


**Figure 9. Advanced Human Control System (HCS) operational model.**

The Primitive Soul and Angelic Soul control loops each receive the same external inputs from the environment and internal feedback from the body. The internal Human Operating System (the two souls) filters and processes these inputs to produce an output response. The output response of the Primitive Soul control loop is connected directly to the body; the body responds to the input from the Primitive Soul by moving or speaking. The Primitive Soul control loop is automatic, almost hard-wired, and it dominates in its control over the actions of the body.

The Angelic Soul control loop, when exercised, can override or influence the actions of the Primitive Soul control loop, but it is not in direct control of the body; only the Primitive Soul is. Therefore, the output of the Angelic Soul control loop may be ignored by the Primitive Soul control loop — and this is how and where the trouble starts with our human nature.

Let's learn more about each of these souls that coexist within us.

## Primitive Soul

The Primitive Soul operates automatically, continuously, and non-stop. Our Primitive Soul operates in a manner similar to gravity; it operates in the background, without any conscious attention, and is ever-present. It is like a computer's device drivers, which are part of the operating system and which control, in the background, the basic, low-level hardware functions. The Primitive Soul performs and controls all automatic, involuntary, and background bodily tasks and handles bodily needs and interests automatically.

For example, when you want to walk across the room, all you need is the intention of moving and a destination. Our Primitive Soul automatically performs all the tasks necessary to activate your bodily functions to create motion, walking, running, or crawling. You do not need any detailed thought about putting one foot in front of the other or in regard to knowing how to keep your body balanced.

Here are the key characteristics of the Primitive Soul (see Appendix A for the Key Soul Characteristics Comparison Table):

- Purpose: Run the body's basic and involuntary functions for survival (protection of self, security, and reproduction)
- Connection: Directly to the body
- Time frame: Now, present time
- Action: Doing, then thinking; does what feels good now — immediate gratification[18]
- Action response: Automatic for involuntary functions; pain response (no thought involved); learned responses
- Human reference: Looks and operates inside the body; "I" or "me"; looks out for self
- Potential: Constant, inflexible; resists change; forms habits; does what it always does

---

18 Immediate gratification — wanting something now without having to work for it first or considering the long-term consequences.

- Right and wrong: Needs laws and boundaries to keep order; experiences conflicts between what is right for self versus what is right for group and society
- Catchphrases: "It's all about me" and "What's in it for me?"
- Ultimate goal: Survival; personal pleasure and satisfaction

## Angelic Soul

The Angelic Soul is truly the piece that makes us different and sets human beings apart from all other living things; it is our unique aspect. Key to being human is our drive for better understanding, of ourselves and of the universe. We do not just take life at face value. We have the desire and the need to explore our inner and outer worlds, and not just for the sake of exploring but for deeper understanding and knowledge so that we can change our world and create a better place for all to live. The Angelic Soul harbors this desire to learn and grow, which is only possible when human beings have the freedom to pursue their desires.

The Angelic Soul (as the Primitive Soul) is part of the operating system installed on a computer. Where each human being sets him- or herself apart from other human beings is with the application programs; these encompass our individual skills and talents that make each person unique (see Figure 4). But, unlike computer applications, we do not get to choose which specific characteristics are downloaded; we are born with our software package — our internal Human Operating System — completely installed. What we do get is the opportunity to expand these skills and talents through our Angelic Soul's ability to learn and grow.

Here are the key characteristics of the Angelic Soul (see Appendix A for the Key Soul Characteristics Comparison Table):

- Purpose: Connect with other souls (relationships) and the universe; experience freedom; learn and grow; love
- Connection: To the infinite and the universe
- Time frame: Past and future

- Action: Thinking, then doing; seeks to do good for now and into the future
- Action response: Calculated, logical, and thought through when dealing with some issues; intuitive, knowing what is right or wrong with other issues
- Human reference: Looks and operates outside the body
- Potential: Open to learning and growth; flexible and adaptable
- Right and wrong: Inherent knowledge of what is right and wrong
- Catchphrase: "Serve the greater good"
- Ultimate goal: Seek out a "greater purpose" for living; contribute to the universe; love; achieve long-term prosperity and happiness

## Soul Boundaries and Limitations

The Primitive Soul deals with the physical limitations and boundaries of the body, and even then sometimes it tries to push the body up against the edges of those limitations and boundaries when attempting to enjoy some of its pleasures. The Primitive Soul can drive the body to do or say anything that satisfies its own needs and desires. Because of these uncontrolled motivations the Primitive Soul needs human-established boundaries and limitations: societal norms, civil laws, and religious dogma. So, we need to understand — *just because we can does not mean we should.* Just because we are able to do something, does not mean doing it is the appropriate[19] thing to do.

The Angelic Soul inherently knows how to interact appropriately with others. It understands and deals with limitations and boundaries as established by humankind, though it does not really need them. This is when the Primitive Soul and Angelic Soul get into conflict: immediate gratification (feels good) versus long-term benefits (does good). This conflict can arise in simple situations, such as whether to eat a candy bar when we are on a restricted diet, whether to leave

---

19 Appropriate — the proper action at the right time and right place.

our dog locked in the car on a hot day, or whether to say something nasty to someone. These events, once we say or do them, we cannot change or recover from. We cannot simply do what we want, when we want to, when acting out of our Primitive Soul side, without facing the consequences of our actions or omissions. Depending on the situation, we may need to live within the established boundaries and limitations.

A corollary to "just because you can does not mean you should" is "do not do what is easy (because it is easy), but rather do what is appropriate." The challenge in most situations is for us to know the difference between *easy* and *appropriate*, and this is where our Angelic Soul comes in. Because the Angelic Soul knows what is best for the greater good and the long-term, it has an inherent sense of what is right or appropriate.

## Time Frames of the Souls

Here is an important detail about the Primitive Soul and Angelic Soul: each soul has a time frame in which it operates. This is crucial to understand, because when life happens and we respond to what is happening, we need to know which soul is doing the responding and which soul *should be* doing the responding.

The Primitive Soul operates in present time. It only knows of events in the here-and-now and only takes action in the here-and-now. Right in the moment, whatever actions we are performing are coming from the Primitive Soul. All the Primitive Soul knows is now, present time.

In contrast, the Angelic Soul operates out of past knowledge and experiences and projects life into the future. The Angelic Soul has a deep understanding of cause and effect; it connects past actions with its current state of happiness and prosperity. Because it can project into the future, it can construct any number of future states (or scenarios) and in that way it brings us hope and faith. The Angelic Soul believes its constructed future state to be true and can then impose these constructed future states on the actions of the Primitive Soul (in present time). The issue or concern with these constructed future states is that they may or may not be logical projections from the present; meaning they can be inconsistent with present circumstances; sometimes called wishful thinking. As an example:

- You "know" (meaning the Angelic Soul projected) that you are going to get that big raise or promotion so you went out and bought a new car and the money never came.
- You have faith your team will complete the project on time, so you don't interfere or ask questions, until it's too late.

When a human being is in immediate danger, the Primitive Soul usually has the best response for survival, because it lives only in present time. In contrast, the long-term health of the body is best left to the Angelic Soul. It connects present circumstances to past actions and to future possibilities, such as understanding the benefits of healthy diet and exercise to long-term health. In contrast, the Primitive Soul knows only of the immediate gratification of eating your favorite candy bar. The Primitive Soul will always pass on starting a new diet and exercise plan today — too much pain and suffering and not enough immediate gratification — whereas the Angelic Soul can project the future and see a fit and healthy person.

Children live in the present. They are not yet aware of a past or a future. They are almost 100 percent living from their Primitive Soul. Their sole experience of life is now and with immediate gratification; they do not understand future consequences. For example, when you tell a child to "Brush your teeth or you will get cavities," the child does not see the connection between cause and effect of brushing teeth to prevent cavities. To communicate to a child's Primitive Soul lifestyle, you might consider telling the child to "Only brush the teeth you want to keep." In this way, the child can see the long-term benefit and realize immediate results — the teeth are clean and still in their mouth.

## Soul Conflict Management

The Human Control System is how we are all "wired." At this point, you have probably noticed that there are many characteristics of the Primitive Soul and the Angelic Soul that run counter to each other. As it turns out, this is the real problem and challenge of being human. This is the curse and the blessing we all struggle with each day. *This* is our human nature.

Once you understand the two-soul concept, human complexity and the seeming dichotomies start to become clearer and make more sense, and they may begin to be more apparent in others and in ourselves. But to be clear: each soul is "good" for its own purposes; one soul is not better than the other. Our Primitive Soul and our Angelic Soul together (along with our body) make us human beings.

When life is happening all around us — some guy cuts you off on the highway, your spouse says "I love you," or your boss is giving you a hard time — the important factor that will make us "better" and happier human beings is your ability to apply the appropriate soul at the appropriate time. We are limited in realizing our potential, improving our relationships, and experiencing our successes only by our inability to apply the appropriate soul response (ASR). Appropriate soul response is the key to our future life successes. Appropriate soul response will change our life. Here are the challenges that limit appropriate soul response:

- Dominant soul: How much we reside in one soul over the other.
- Soul flow: The degree that we can easily move or flow between souls.

## Dominant Soul

The difficulties and challenges of life occur when the Primitive Soul and the Angelic Soul have counter objectives for a particular event or when the soul response you offer is not the most appropriate for the circumstances. Unfortunately, there is no third party to select responses or arbitrate between the two souls — it is still you. What makes appropriate soul response challenging is that each of us has a natural leaning toward one soul or the other, our dominant soul. This natural leaning and its degree are different for each person. Most people unconsciously lean toward their Primitive Soul because of its automatic, protective nature (see Figure 10).

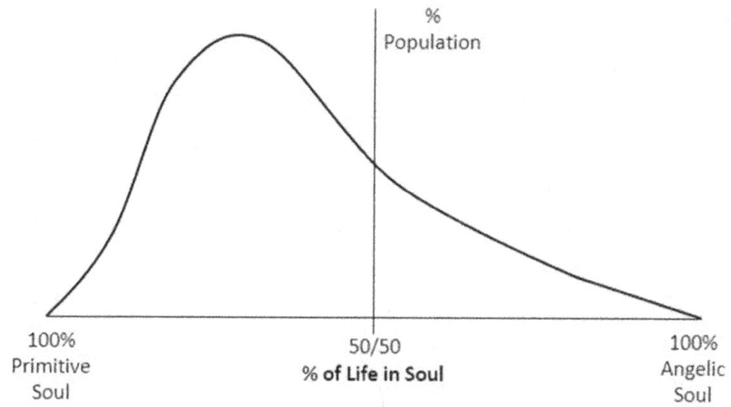


**Figure 10. General Population Soul Distribution Spectrum** — *skewed toward the dominant Primitive Soul (estimated).*

## Soul Flow

We are a combination of both souls, but one soul is dominant, and most likely it is our Primitive Soul. This normal tendency does not limit us at any moment in time from acting from either soul. However, to have appropriate soul response, we must be able to *freely* choose the appropriate soul to respond with. An appropriate soul response can occur only when we can easily move or flow between our souls, and most people need to have their Angelic Soul act to offset the constant effects of their Primitive Soul. The Angelic Soul has to force itself into present time to address the constant drive of the Primitive Soul. Therefore, for appropriate soul response, our objective is to achieve a conscious choosing and free flow between our Primitive Soul and our Angelic Soul as required by circumstances — soul flow.

Next, we get into the details of the mechanisms of the internal Human Operating System to provide insight into how and why you act and respond in certain ways in certain circumstances.

## Key Takeaways

1. The internal Human Operating System brings life and purpose to the body.
2. The human soul is the internal Human Operating System and comprises the Primitive Soul and the Angelic Soul.
3. The complete Human Control System operational model includes the body (with its input sensors and output devices) driven by the two cascaded control loops of the internal Human Operating System — the Primitive Soul and the Angelic Soul.
4. The Primitive Soul is connected to the body, and the Angelic Soul is connected to the universe.
5. Within the Human Control System, the goals and objectives of the Primitive Soul and Angelic Soul influence us differently because each soul has a different group of motivational factors.
6. The Primitive Soul output response is limited by the hard capabilities of our body and the natural laws of the universe, and the Angelic Soul output response is limited by the soft dictates established by humankind through societal norms, civil laws, and religious dogma.
7. The Primitive Soul's catchphrases are "It's all about me" and "What's in it for me?"
8. The Angelic Soul's catchphrase is "To serve the greater good."
9. The real problem and challenge of being human is reconciling the opposing and counter-purpose characteristics of the Primitive Soul and the Angelic Soul.
10. Appropriate soul response is the key to life successes. Appropriate soul response will change your life.
11. To establish appropriate soul response, we need to achieve soul flow, the ability to *freely* move or flow between our two souls.

# CHAPTER 7

# MOTIVATIONAL FACTORS OF THE PRIMITIVE SOUL

*Individual man, shielded by civilization against the elementary dangers of life, is ordinarily free of the need to maintain a primitive state of alertness. Yet the ways of the animal world still hold a strange fascination for us, and men periodically feel compelled to return to the exposed life of the forest and the sea.*
— Dr. Smiley Blanton, psychoanalyst

EACH SOUL HAS ITS UNIQUE purpose within our body. This purpose then drives us to perform and respond to life in a certain manner. The drive consists of specific groups of motivational factors. The Primitive Soul's groups of motivational factors are:
- Abundance and Prosperity
- Pain and Pleasure
- Identity and Belonging

Because of the Primitive Soul's relationship to the body, all Primitive Soul motivational factors support the needs and desires of the body. Some bodily needs and desires are so basic to our existence that they are considered "animalistic," similar to those of an animal. The Primitive Soul's animalistic motivational factors are all based on the fundamental motivation of survival:

- Food and eating: To hunt, farm, or gather all the necessary food and water to survive
- Safety and shelter: To get out of the weather, to keep warm, and to stay safe from danger
- Sex and reproduction: To create a family, affiliate with other humans, and perpetuate the species

But we are human; once these animalistic bodily needs are fulfilled, we go beyond them to fulfill the Primitive Soul's "humanistic" bodily needs. The Primitive Soul's humanistic motivational factors are as follows:

- Clothing: To protect the body from the environment and to keep warm
- Grooming and beautifying: To keep clean and healthy and to make the body more attractive so as to attract a mate
- Self-indulgence: To do whatever we want for pure pleasure, entertainment, or gratification

These are all significant motivational factors for the "it's all about me" Primitive Soul.

## Abundance and Prosperity

As it turns out, food and eating, safety and shelter, sex and reproduction, clothing, grooming and beautifying, and self-indulgence are all factors of the first Primitive Soul motivational group, Abundance and Prosperity. Abundance and Prosperity motivational factors range on a continuum, from food and eating to self-indulgence; this continuum is called the Prosperity Progression, as shown in Figure 11. One objective of the Primitive Soul is to drive us up the Prosperity Progression.

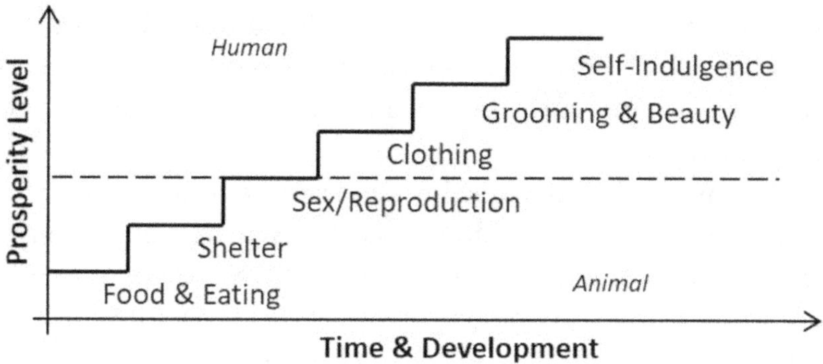


**Figure 11. Primitive Soul motivation to drive us up the Prosperity Progression.**

A free[20] human being naturally pursues abundance and prosperity. We will naturally move toward getting more on the Prosperity Progression and move away from anything that limits or attempts to limit our ability to achieve these objectives.

What you see in the Abundance and Prosperity motivational group is that the ultimate goal of the Primitive Soul is beyond simple survival (the desire to be safe, secure, warm, and protected); the ultimate goal of the Primitive Soul is to be happy and fulfilled, with abundance and prosperity. But this form of happiness and fulfillment is from a materialistic standpoint, achieving the desires of the body, such as wanting lots of stuff and many things (fancy cars, big homes, jewelry, and other toys) — all the stuff that satisfies your bodily needs. Once we satisfy these basic needs, we move up the Prosperity Progression to self-indulgent activities, the "fun stuff."

However, as human beings, our goal should not be simply to move up the Prosperity Progression but to move up from one level to the next, achieving stability and abundance at each level before

---

20 Free — unobstructed by outside rules, laws, social norms, influences, cages, or confines.

moving to the next level. On the Prosperity Progression continuum, the order of obtainment and stability are extremely important. When a person obtains the first level and is stable there, then that person (group or society) can move up to obtain stability at the next level, and so on. The Primitive Soul directive is to keep the body safe and fed (animalistic motivations), and then to seek self-indulgence (humanistic motivations).

One form of self-indulgence is entertainment, what we do to fill the time when we are not doing necessary activities like earning a living, learning new skills and information, or taking care of our shelter or the people around us. Some say this is useful time, to take our minds off the obligations and responsibilities of life and to "let our batteries recharge." All forms of entertainment — whether it is gambling, sports, computer/video games, theater, movies, radio, television, horseracing, cock fights, etc. — fall into two categories: participatory and spectator. From the Primitive Soul perspective, entertainment *is* happiness.

Self-indulgence by definition is problematic for an organized society because its focus is on *self*. A highly self-indulgent person lacks discipline and has an inability to resist excessive or unrestrained gratification of his or her appetites, desires, passions, whims, or sexual pleasures. In general, self-indulgent behaviors and activities are focused on what we consider luxury items — not life's necessities — those things that bring about immediate pleasure or gratification, to excess, without restraint, limits, or any regard for future consequences.

## Pain and Pleasure

Associated with the need to survive, the Primitive Soul motivates us with the physical and emotional drives of pain and pleasure — more specifically, pain avoidance (less of this) and pleasure seeking (more of this). This is the second Primitive Soul motivational group: Pain and Pleasure.

## Avoiding Pain

Pain is both physical and emotional. Physical pain involves the infliction of harm on the body, and emotional pain includes situations or events that make us feel uncomfortable or unpleasantly challenged. Pain avoidance has benefits and consequences, pluses and minuses.

Physical pain is real in the sense that an internal or external stimulus interacts negatively on the body and could actually damage it. When the body is presented with a clear and present danger, the action to avoid the pain is usually the most appropriate. However, in some cases pain may be of benefit — for example, pushing the body to an existing physical limit provides the opportunity to discover greater ability and reward. Sometimes our greatest achievements are on the other side of a wall of pain, such as giving birth or completing a marathon; hence the expression "no pain, no gain."

The subject of emotional pain is less concrete than that of physical pain. Emotional pain is a construct of the Primitive Soul; it occurs when the Primitive Soul is in conflict with the Angelic Soul or when Primitive Soul motivational factors are threatened. Because the Primitive Soul has a close relationship with the body, emotional pain can also manifest as physical issues (though the physical issues are not the original source of the pain). As with physical pain, there may be great benefit in pushing through emotional pain and discovering greater potential or healing.

All emotional pain is self-inflicted. We cannot be subjected to emotional pain without our consent. Say someone *hurts our feelings* by saying something we do not like or agree with. This affliction of emotional pain occurs when past unresolved and buried internal issues or problems are brought back into the present and we have to deal with them again (more on this later). And this is a distinct characteristic of emotional pain: because we grant it the right to exist, we can also then reduce its impact, get rid of it, or prevent it from coming into existence in the first place.

## Seeking Pleasure

To the Primitive Soul-motivated human being, seeking pleasure is almost always analogous to happiness. In pleasure seeking, we want unchecked access to all levels of the Prosperity Progression and specifically self-indulgence — call it extreme pleasure seeking. This even includes jumping around the Prosperity Progression, to enjoy whatever you want whenever you want it. Pleasure seeking is most certainly rewarding to the body and the Primitive Soul; it feels good. Physical and emotional pleasures give us immediate fulfillment and make us feel happy.

Our Primitive Soul motivates us to jump quickly up the Prosperity Progression. Jumping up and jumping around the levels on the Prosperity Progression provide immediate gratification. Immediate gratification means getting something *now* without having to work for it or (more problematic) having it without creating a stable prosperity foundation and without concern for the long-term consequences of our actions and desires. Immediate gratification does not create stability from level to level, and therefore it does not produce long-term happiness. It is most certainly catastrophic to jump to "self-indulgence" and fake being stable there. The urge for immediate gratification provides short-term gain, pleasure, and a sense or feeling of prosperity but at the risk of long-term problems, instability, and personal failure.

## Identity and Belonging

The third Primitive Soul motivational group is Identity and Belonging. Unlike animals, which desire to be either alone or associated with a group or pack, human beings are motivated for both. This drives our need to being both an individual, with a unique identity, and our need to fit in and belong to a group of some kind.

## Finding Identity

Your unique identity is the holy trinity — not the "father, son, and Holy Ghost" one — of me, myself, and I. Your identity is the long list of personal characteristics that make you *you*, unique, one of a kind, and different. Identity could be the most significant of all Primitive Soul motivational factors. It is how we each see ourselves; it is how we create distinction between us and the billions of other human beings. We project our personal identity for everyone to see in everything we do and say. Sometimes our identity sticks out even before we say a word, by the clothes we wear, the car we drive, or the way we cut or wear our hair or decorate our body.

In the beginning, our parents created our first identity: our birth date and name (and some other things you might be going to the therapist for). Many people get excited when you remember and acknowledge their birthday and most people are offended when you get their name wrong. These are the first things we learn about ourselves as children, about our identity; and then, after that, we learn whether we are a boy or a girl. These are the big first three; after these, the list of personal identity characteristics (PICs) varies for each of us.

We even created rituals around our identity to reinforce it, such as birthday parties, club or organization initiations, religious services and symbols, and holiday parades. Each of us has a unique and specific set of personal identity characteristics to describe ourselves. Here is a partial list of some common personal identity characteristics:

- Name: First, last, maybe both, nickname
- Birth date: Birth year or month, astrological sign, generation (Baby Boomer, Gen X, Millennial)
- Sex: Male/female, transgender, bisexual, homosexual
- Body: Skinny, fat, in shape, tall, short, birthmarks, deformities
- Appearance: Hair color, long hair, short hair, no hair, complexion, clothing style
- Ethnicity: Country of origin

- Race: Caucasoid (White), Negroid (Black), Mongoloid (Asian), mixed race
- Religion: Christian, Muslim, Jew, Buddhist, Hindu, atheist, agnostic
- Place of birth: City, state, country
- Who/what parents did: Doctor, lawyer, salesperson, teacher, white collar, blue collar, no collar, reputation
- Family/family history and heritage: Children, mother, father, siblings, "I am my mother's daughter," "I am not my father," family origin, DNA
- Perfection: Can do no wrong, cannot do right
- Profession: Doctor, lawyer, salesperson, teacher, white collar, blue collar, no collar
- Net worth: Rich, poor, middle-class
- Character: Good, bad, honest, sinner, saint
- Education/intelligence: PhD, Mensa member, school of hard knocks, IQ
- Schooling: Ivy League, private, public
- Food/diet: Vegetarian, vegan, gluten-free, blood type
- Car: Color, make, model, sports car, truck, electric
- Pet(s): Dog, cat, exotic pet
- Organizations: Membership, fraternity, sorority, clubs
- Political party: Democrat, Republican, Libertarian, Independent, Green, Communist, Socialist
- Sports team(s): College, professional, baseball, soccer
- Activities: Golf, tennis, soccer, bowling, cycling, rock climbing
- Hobbies: Quilting, rock collecting, cooking, ham radio
- Struggles and challenges: Cancer survivor, alcoholism, disability, abusive parent, gender identity
- Coffee you drink: Brand, size, and flavor, including when and how often, cannot start the day without it

As you see, this list of personal identity characteristics is lengthy, and I am sure you can add several more. The important thing about your list is that it is unique to you and that you are motivated to create and maintain an identity and self-image that is indeed different from others' and one of a kind.

Personal identity characteristics run the spectrum from strong to weak. Strong characteristics are so much you that without them you would not be you, starting with your name and your birthday. The strength of the other personal identity characteristics can be tested by noting your reaction to changing, removing, or replacing them.

Here is the problem and challenge regarding personal identity characteristics: our identity both defines who we are and limits us at the same time. The greater our attachment is to any one characteristic, the greater the restriction on our ability to change and grow. The more we say, "I am __________," the less opportunity we have to be anyone else — even a different and better person. The more strongly we cling to our personal identity characteristics, the more inflexible we become; the more we are repeatedly trapped by our identity, such as by our self-interests, beliefs, and prejudices, the less likely we are to make appropriate and rational decisions and choices, and the more we are forced to defend our identity and inappropriate or irrational positions and opinions on anything we identify with.

> *"It gives you a façade that you can show the world, but it also turns into a shield behind which you hide."*
> Deepak Chopra

## *Exercise Break*

Start a list of your personal identity characteristics. Begin your list with the characteristics listed above and add any others that you can think of. Keep asking and answering the question, "I am __________." Keep the list of your personal identity characteristics going continually; more identity characteristics will come up as you start to observe yourself. Hold on to this list because we get back to it later.

## Needing to Belong

Almost as strong as our impulse to carve out a personal identity and our drive to defend it is our need to fit in and belong to some kind of pack, group, family, club, gang, organization, or team. We need and want to be a part of something bigger than ourselves, something we can identify with. We want to associate with or be a member of groups and organizations that have interests and objectives in common with ours. Some people have even faked their identity to fit into a group. The group setting offers safety in numbers, shared experiences, a learning environment, common expression, comfort, and membership. In some ways the other human beings involved in the group are the same as you.

> *"Why fit in when you were born to stand out?"*
> Dr. Seuss

Groups we affiliate with have their own set of unique personal identity characteristics. So, even though we transfer our individual, personal identity to the group when we join it, we can maintain our individual uniqueness through the unique group identity that sets it apart from other groups. Affiliation with the group now becomes part of our own list of personal identity characteristics.

Herein lies the problem and challenge with the Identity and Belonging motivational group: negotiating the dichotomy of maintaining a unique identity and fitting into a group. On one hand, you are told to be yourself, and on the other hand, you are told that there is no *I* in team, there is no room for the individual, you have to fit in, and you need to belong to the group or the community. Sometimes we want to be like the lone wolf stalking its prey — alone, unique (the "I"); other times we want to be like a sheep — just one of the herd, the same as everyone else (the team). Though we are constantly asked about our identity and pressured to be different, this is in opposition to the directive to "be yourself," and that is why you cannot just fit in. We spend a lot of time and effort trying to distance ourselves from the people around us, but then we want to be just like them.

The bottom line with identity and belonging is: for us there is not a right way or wrong way to be, only the proper way. As mentioned earlier, choosing the proper way to be depends on the many in-the-moment conditions and circumstances and the long-term results we want to achieve. Sometimes standing out from the crowd is the proper way to go (like dressing for a comic book convention) and other times fitting into the group (like running a relay race).

## Key Takeaways

1. The Primitive Soul motivational factor groups are as follows:
   - Abundance and Prosperity
   - Pain and Pleasure
   - Identity and Belonging
2. The ultimate goals of the Primitive Soul are me-oriented: pleasure and control and power over things and other human beings.
3. Abundance and Prosperity: The ultimate goal of the Primitive Soul is to be happy and fulfilled, from a materialistic standpoint, by moving up the Prosperity Progression to self-indulgent and by fulfilling the desires of the body for lots of fun and stuff.
4. Pain and Pleasure: We strive for pain avoidance and pleasure seeking.
   - Avoid Pain. Pain can be both physical and emotional. Physical pain involves the infliction of harm on the body, and emotional pain is when we feel uncomfortable or unpleasantly challenged. Physical pain could bring actual damage to the body, so physical pain avoidance is usually warranted. Emotional pain is a construct of the Primitive Soul and occurs when the Primitive Soul is in conflict with the Angelic Soul or when other Primitive Soul motivational factors are threatened.
   - Pleasure seeking. In pleasure seeking we want unchecked access to all the levels on the Prosperity Progression, to enjoy whatever we want whenever we want it. Pleasure seeking

feels good. The urge for immediate gratification provides short-term gain, pleasure, and a sense or feeling of prosperity, but at the risk of long-term problems, instability, and personal failure.

5.  Identity and Belonging: The challenge with identity and belonging is handling the dichotomy of trying to be unique while trying to fit in.

    - Finding identity. Identity could be the most significant of the Primitive Soul motivational factors. Personal identity characteristics make each of us unique human beings. But our identity both defines us and limits us. The greater our attachment to any one personal identity characteristic, the more limited we are to change and grow and the less opportunity we have to be anyone else.

    - Needing to belong. The need to fit in and belong to some kind of group is a strong motivational factor. We want to be part of something bigger than ourselves, something we can identify with.

# CHAPTER 8

# MOTIVATIONAL FACTORS OF THE ANGELIC SOUL

*It is a tragedy of the world that no one knows
what he doesn't know — and the less a man knows,
the more sure he is that he knows everything.*
— Joyce Cary, Art and Reality

WHAT TRULY MAKE HUMAN BEINGS unique in this world are our Angelic Soul motivational factors. They are distinct and unrelated to the body. All Angelic Soul motivational factors support the needs and desires of the human being to understand and connect to (be in relationship with) the greater whole — the universe and all its souls. The Angelic Soul's groups of motivational factors are:

- Purpose and Meaning
- Knowledge and Creativity
- Peace and Love

The true objective of the universe is simple: to create a sense of (w)holiness — a sense of unity and oneness in the world and among the souls it contains. The sense of (w)holiness is based on the fundamental motivation for unity (oneness) and peace, the longing for all souls to live in peace and harmony together. (W)holiness is brought about when the focus is on what is best for the greater good.

Until we raise our awareness, most people are predominately motivated by their Primitive Soul. We struggle up the Prosperity Progression, trying to make it to the top and feeling good about our successes. What we do not realize yet is that when we finally get to the top of the Prosperity Progression — to self-indulgence — there is nowhere else to go and we are left with the ultimate dilemma. You see, just living out of our Primitive Soul and working our way up the Prosperity Progression is self-centric, finite, and limited. We are left with a meaningless existence of self-indulgence.

## Purpose and Meaning

However, when we learn to live out of our Angelic Soul, we are led in a different direction, a more rewarding and fulfilling direction. The first group of motivational factors of the Angelic Soul is to find Purpose and Meaning to our life and our living. The Angelic Soul keeps us asking the "big" questions: What is the purpose of my life? What am I going to do to make my life worth living? The Angelic Soul motivates us to search out a purpose and meaning for our life that is bigger than us as individuals and that is not focused on our needs as individuals. A purpose and meaning that connects us with the universe, with other souls, and the infinite, God, a higher spirit. Through this connection we find an understanding of the universe and of ourselves.

> *"The purpose of life is to discover your gift. The work of life is to develop it. The meaning of life is to give your gift away."*
> David Viscott

The Angelic Soul motivates us not only to create big and lofty purposes but also to bring purpose and meaning to the most mundane parts of life, our relationships and work, because this is where we spend most of our time living.

The Angelic Soul drives us to live a life of purpose and meaning. In the end, the ultimate and purest form of happiness comes from a life that is directed by a purpose and filled with meaning, not a collection of things and stuff.

## Knowledge and Creativity

The second group of motivational factors of the Angelic Soul is to pursue Knowledge and Creativity. In the pursuit of knowledge and creativity, all things in the universe are possible. Knowledge and creativity are the enabling forces of self-discovery and learning. The more we access knowledge and creativity, the more we question what we know and believe, the more we grow and understand, and the less we lean on our existing personal identity characteristics.

## Knowledge

Knowledge is of three types: the stuff you *know*, the stuff you *know you do not know*, and the stuff you *do not know you do not know* (see Figure 12). The amount of stuff you *know* is very clear — you know it — and it is finite. Even the stuff you *do not know* is clear — you know you do not know it — and that is finite, too. But the stuff you *do not know you do not know* — now that is unclear and unknown — and that is potentially infinite, because we human beings discover and learn new information about ourselves and our universe almost daily.

> *"To know is to know that you know nothing. That is the meaning of true knowledge."*
> Socrates

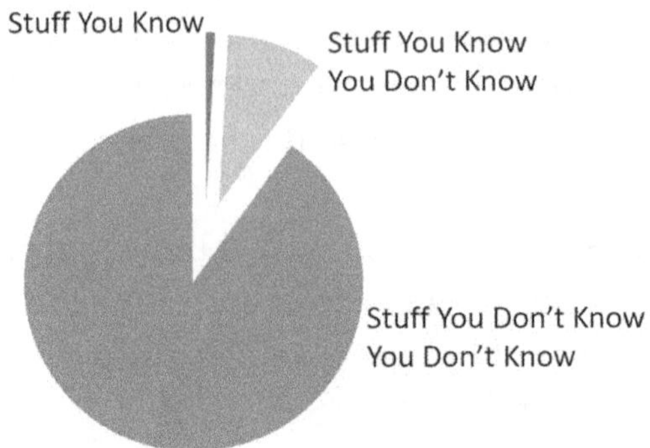


**Figure 12. Pie of knowledge.**
Proportions vary person to person.

So, what is the stuff you *know*? You know the language this book is written in, you know your family, you may even know how to drive a car or fish, and you know many other skills, information, and ideas. What is the stuff you *do not know*? Perhaps how to fly a helicopter, how to solve a Rubik's Cube, calculus, who shot J. R., and much else, but you know you do not know these things, and you do know these things exist and you can choose to learn them or continue not knowing them.

The issue with knowledge is how we store and access it. We store knowledge by categories in defined "knowledge buckets," such as buckets for language, mathematics, physical activities, sports statistics, and art, as shown in Figure 13. And when we acquire new knowledge in an area we already know something about, we store the new knowledge in an existing knowledge bucket. For knowledge we *know we do not know*, and because we know these topics exist, we have a knowledge bucket already, but the knowledge bucket is empty.

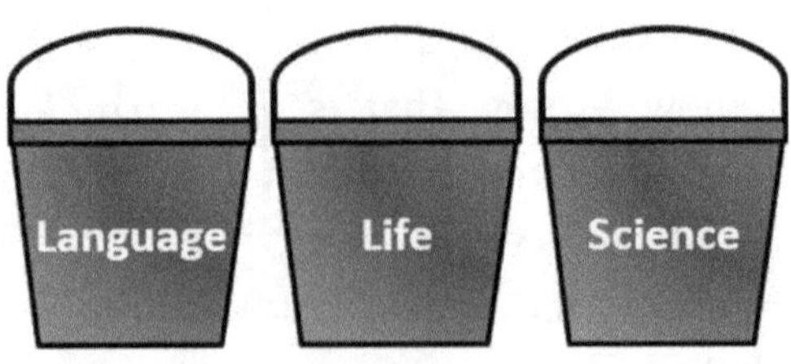


**Figure 13. Knowledge buckets.**

But what about the stuff you *do not know you do not know*? As of today, you have no clue these things even exist. For some, the information in this book might have been totally unknown until they started reading, and now they know they did not know it existed before they picked up the book. The real question with any unknown knowledge is how we fit it into our lives when we come to know it, and which knowledge bucket we put it in within our finite set of knowledge buckets.

When information is presented from the area of stuff *you did not know you did not know*, we have two choices of what to do with it:

1) Put it in an existing knowledge bucket, or

2) Create a new knowledge bucket and put it in there.

When we put newfound information in an existing knowledge bucket, we treat it like stuff we already know. We do not give it any special regard, and that could be a mistake. The Angelic Soul motivates us to pursue information and knowledge, which means that we have the opportunity to view all new information as unique and to create new knowledge buckets when necessary to allow this new knowledge to affect our lives in new ways. Otherwise, Isaac Newton may have overlooked the falling apple as just a nuisance.

> *"To know what you know and what you do not know, that is true knowledge."*
> Confucius

## Creativity

The motivation to pursue creativity drives us to beautify and improve the physical environment around us, at home and at work. We accomplish this through art, music, literature, woodworking, cooking, sewing, engineering, and in many other ways. The creativity motivation also drives us to beautify and improve our emotional environments, in all our relationships.

Creativity is almost the opposite of knowledge. Knowledge is discovering what already exists, whereas creativity is producing something that has not yet existed. However, creativity is not possible without knowledge, and creativity (like knowledge) brings the world of the unknown into the world of the known.

The pursuit of creativity is the motivation that really sets human beings apart from all other living creatures. Collectively, our drive to create in the last hundred years has produced some of the most amazing things — some very bad and some very good. But, overall, what human beings have created has made the world a better place to live in by enabling us to climb

> *"Creativity involves breaking out of established patterns in order to look at things in a different way."*
> Edward de Bono

the Prosperity Progression. We have created language, and through language we have created poetry, song, and literature. We have created art and architecture. We have created the sciences to study how the world works.

The combination of knowledge and creativity enables human beings to access the wonders and beauty of the universe. With the creativity motivation, we bring about change; without change the world would cease to grow and we would fail to achieve our purpose. Change through the power of creativity also gives human beings the ability to adapt, and adaptation enables human beings to survive and to access the infinite possibilities of the universe. When our creative motivation is fully actualized, we reach our full and intended potential. Creativity arises when we listen with new ears, look with new eyes, and speak with a new mouth.

## Peace and Love

The third group of motivational factors of the Angelic Soul is to live with Peace and Love. However, the key to achieving Peace and Love is that it requires at least two human beings to participate. The motivation of Peace and Love requires us to

> *"It takes two to make peace."*
> John F. Kennedy

get beyond our body, because peace and love can occur only between two or more souls. The selfless Angelic Soul motivation of Peace and Love counteracts the selfishness of the Primitive Soul.

Of all the Angelic Soul motivations, Peace and Love seems to be the most difficult for human beings to achieve, at least on the macro level. When we look around, we see a lot of war and hate, killing and anger. How could it be such a strong motivational factor when all this mayhem continues? Well, consider it this way: if it were not such a strong motivating factor, we would not be upset by all the strife we see around us. It also highlights how much our Primitive Soul influences our daily activities and how much attention we need to put on allowing our Angelic Soul to counter-influence us.

Peace and love are the highest goals of the Angelic Soul, and the pathway to peace and love is friendship, which leads to brotherhood/ sisterhood, which leads to unity, then to peace, and finally to complete and pure love. To truly love someone else requires us to act from our Angelic Soul. When we act from our Primitive Soul, we only know love of self and material things. Only the Angelic Soul can connect with another soul, whether animal or human. Only the Angelic Soul can connect with the beauty of the world — the awesomeness of a waterfall, the grandeur of a landscape, the peace and romance of a sunset. The Peace and Love motivation is behind our affinity for people, animals, and the beauty of nature. Ultimate human happiness occurs when we are at peace and in love.

> *"Darkness cannot drive out darkness; only light can do that. Hate cannot drive out hate; only love can do that."*
> Martin Luther King, Jr.

## *Key Takeaways*

1. The Angelic Soul motivational factor groups are as follows:
   - Purpose and Meaning
   - Knowledge and Creativity
   - Peace and Love

2. The ultimate goals of the Angelic Soul are finding and pursuing purpose and love.

3. Purpose and Meaning: The Angelic Soul motivates us to search for a purpose and for meaning in our lives that are bigger than us and not about just us as individuals. The purest form of happiness comes from a life lived with meaning and purpose, a purpose and meaning that connect us with the universe and with other souls.

4. Knowledge and Creativity: The more we access knowledge and creativity, the more we question what we know and believe, the more we grow and understand, and the less we lean on our existing personal identity characteristics.

   - Knowledge comes as three types: the stuff we know, the stuff we know we do not know, and the stuff we do not know we do not know. We store knowledge in defined knowledge buckets by categories. Looking at all new information as unique and creating new knowledge buckets when necessary allows new information and knowledge to affect our lives in new ways.

   - Creativity is the act of producing something that has not yet existed. The creativity motivation allows us to effect change, and without change the world ceases to grow and we fail to achieve our purpose. Change through the power of creativity also gives human beings the ability to adapt.

5. Peace and Love: The Peace and Love motivation requires us to get beyond our body, because peace and love can only occur between two or more souls. To truly love someone requires us to act from our Angelic Soul because only the Angelic Soul can connect with another soul. The pathway to peace and love is friendship, brotherhood/sisterhood, unity, peace, and finally love. The ultimate of human happiness occurs when we are at peace and in love.

6. We need to have our Angelic Soul have greater influence on our lives.

# WHAT DOES IT ALL MEAN?

# CHAPTER 9

# SOUL SOLUTIONS

*An old Cherokee told his grandson, "My son, there's a battle between two wolves inside us all. One is Evil. It is anger, jealousy, greed, resentment, inferiority, lies, and ego. The other is Good. It is joy, peace, love, hope, humility, kindness, and truth." The boy thought about it, and asked, "Grandfather, which one wins?" The old man quietly replied, "The one you feed."*

NOW WE HAVE SEEN THE details of the Human Control System operational model and learned about the internal Human Operating System (iHOS). Within the internal Human Operating System there are two distinct souls — the Primitive Soul and the Angelic Soul. Each soul has its own set of characteristics, motivations, and purpose in how it exists and interacts with the real world (see Appendix A). Having these two souls is what makes us distinctly human.

We do not have a choice in regard to having two souls, nor about which one Soul we would like to have instead of the other. Being human means that each soul has an appropriate time and place to be dominant, and knowing when to allow the appropriate soul to prevail is what makes us better, happier, and more productive human beings.

## Soul Response

As the world around us changes, we need to learn how to change our response and how we interact with it. Most likely we are no longer struggling each day to survive the unforgiving world around us — to protect ourselves and our family, to fight our way to the top of the pecking-order to have food to eat. Though some people in the world still fight for daily survival, probably we are not one of them. Because we have achieved a higher level on the Prosperity Progression and our basic survival needs are secured; as such, we can now learn more effective ways to respond and interact with the real world, or more specifically, with the other souls around us.

When life comes at us, we need to *actively* choose the appropriate soul response; otherwise, we revert automatically to our naturally dominant soul response. This means almost all people go to their Primitive Soul first, without even considering the alternative of an Angelic Soul response. But as human beings, we do have the freedom of choice in how we react in each moment of each day — if and only if we wake up and consider the alternatives before we talk or act (more on this later).

It is hard to create a sense of (w)holiness with the universe when most people lean so hard over to the Primitive Soul side of life. Look around. Lots of people operate from their Primitive Soul and spend little time operating from their Angelic Soul. There are exceptions, those who naturally operate more from their Angelic Soul side. Regardless, now it is time for you to open up to choosing the appropriate soul response. Each soul has an appropriate place and time to direct your behavior. When necessary, you must override the auto-response mode of the Primitive Soul with an Angelic Soul response.

## Soul Perception

Each soul drives our behavior, interactions, and response patterns in specific directions. Our behaviors, interactions, and responses are the sum total of how we have expressed our Primitive Soul and Angelic Soul motivations. The two souls' motivating factors influence how we see and perceive the world.

## A Primitive Soul-Influenced World

How Primitive Soul-motivated people perceive the world is directly related to how they perceive themselves. Because they are motivated by abundance and prosperity and seek to move up the Prosperity Progression, they are driven to acquire and consume lots of stuff. To other human beings, this behavior appears greedy or overly ambitious. Primitive Soul-motivated people are also driven to avoid pain and to obtain pleasure. To other human beings, this behavior appears lazy or unmotivated. They are also driven to create a strong identity for themselves. To other human beings, this appears egotistical, self-centered, selfish, cliquish, elitist, and arrogant. Our unique behavior is a specific combination of all of these.

Primitive Soul-motivated people see the world a certain way. They see other human beings as they see themselves: as self-absorbed. So, Primitive Soul-motivated people perceive other human beings as untrustworthy, incompetent, lacking empathy, and selfish. All these behaviors, interactions, and responses are based around the catchphrase "It's all about me" or "What's in it for me?" and the other key characteristics of the Primitive Soul.

What then happens is that highly Primitive Soul-motivated people see and believe the whole world is just like them. Deep down, Primitive Soul-motivated people know they are in it for themselves, so they believe every other person is the same way, and they see and treat others with that in mind. They see everyone as greedy, selfish, arrogant bastards who, therefore, cannot be trusted or believed; they are out for themselves and have a sense of entitlement.

## An Angelic Soul-Influenced World

How Angelic Soul-motivated people perceive the world is also directly related to how they perceive themselves. Because they are motivated to seek purpose and meaning in their lives, they are driven to constantly ask the big and tough questions about who they are and why they are here. To other human beings, this behavior makes them appear as if they are contemplative or sometimes lost. Angelic Soul-motivated people pursue knowledge and creativity. To other human beings, this makes them appear as smart or innovative. And they seek peace and love in the world. To other human beings, this behavior makes them appear like flower children or great companions. Our unique behavior is a specific combination of all of these plus the Primitive Soul ones.

Angelic Soul-motivated people see the world in a certain way, also. They see other human beings as they see themselves: as ambassadors of peace and love. So they perceive other human beings as loving and kind, trustworthy, and concerned for others' well-being. All these behaviors, interactions, and responses are based around the catchphrase "To serve the greater good" and the other key characteristics of the Angelic Soul.

What then happens is that highly Angelic Soul-motivated people see and believe the whole world is just like them. Deep down, Angelic Soul-motivated people know they are in it to care for others, so they believe every other person is doing the same, and they treat and see others with that in mind. They see everyone as involved, caring, thoughtful angels who, therefore, can be trusted and left alone to care for the world; they are very giving of themselves and humble.

## Soul Act

The key to your success as a son or daughter, sister or brother, husband or wife, mother or father, boss or employee, or human being is knowing which soul to act out of and when and, most importantly, knowing that you have the freedom to choose which soul to act from. To know this, you must understand humankind's purpose and your individual purpose for being here: Are you here to get only what you want, or are you here to create a meaningful impact on the people around you and to leave the world a better place?

Strength and long-term success in life come from wrestling with the constant need to learn and choose which soul to act from in each moment of each day that will bring the greatest good — peace and happiness. Living life with the freedom to choose and the choices we make is the biggest challenge, but that is where we must live.

Now it is time to put some real-life experiences to the Human Control System operational model and the internal Human Operating System to see how our Primitive Soul and our Angelic Soul deal with them:

- Communication and conversation
- Feelings and emotions
- Guilty feelings
- Give and take
- Relationships and trust
- Free will, free choice, and self-control
- Living in your own world

## Key Takeaways

1. Do not let ourselves go to our automatic, dominant soul response; actively choose the appropriate soul response (which soul dominates in the appropriate place at the appropriate time).
2. We have the freedom to choose how we react each moment of each day when we can consider the alternatives of which soul to allow being in control before we speak or act.
3. Each soul sees the world in a certain way:
   a) Primitive Soul-motivated people see everyone as greedy, selfish, arrogant bastards.
   b) Angelic Soul-motivated people see everyone as involved, caring, thoughtful angels.
4. Know you have a choice and exercise the Angelic Soul's capability to override the auto-response mode of the Primitive Soul when appropriate.
5. Ask yourself every day and all day, "So, which soul am I going to feed today?"

# CHAPTER 10

# COMMUNICATION AND CONVERSATION

*The two words "information" and "communication" are often used interchangeably, but they signify quite different things. Information is giving out; communication is getting through.*
— Sydney J. Harris, American journalist

CONSIDER THIS: TWO PEOPLE, JOAN and Fred, are having a conversation. Joan wants Fred to do something for her. The only way Fred is going to know what Joan wants is for Joan to successfully transfer her idea to Fred. This is the concept of how real communication works, whether verbal (talking face-to-face, using two tin cans with a long string, telephone, or video chat), written (in the form of cave painting, smoke signals, carrier pigeon, letters, email, or text), body language, telepathic, turn signals, or other non-verbal forms. The objective and purpose of real communication is the successful transfer of a message (information or ideas) from one person (the sender) to another person (the receiver) (see Figure 14). An extension of the communication-cycle model is conversation, the back-and-forth exchange of messages between two or more people.

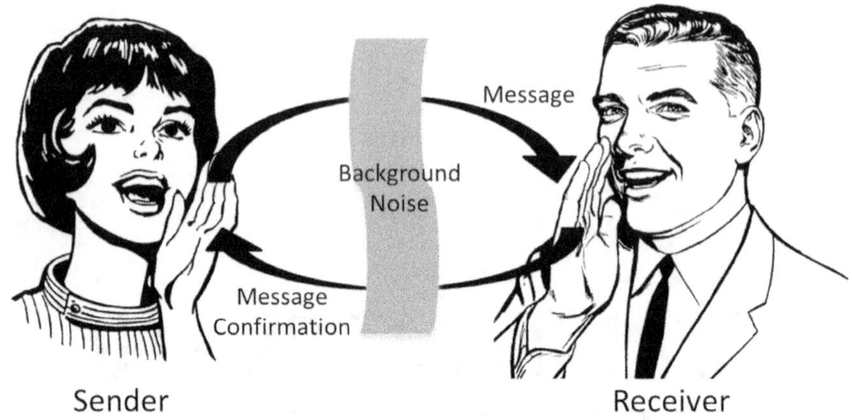


**Figure 14. Successful communication-cycle model.**

Successful communication is more than a one-way data link. If Joan was to yell some information over to Fred and then turn around and walk away, that could not be classified as a successful communication-cycle. Joan cannot be sure that she was heard by Fred or that her message was received correctly. He may have heard Joan say something but might not comprehend the message because he was busy doing something else or there was too much background noise.

A successful communication-cycle requires that the sender (Joan, in this case) validates the message was received correctly by the receiver (Fred). It is the *responsibility of the sender* to ensure that the message is received correctly, not the receiver's. After all, the sender wants to transmit the message in the first place, and only the sender really knows what the true and correct message is.

> *"The single biggest problem in communication is the illusion that it has taken place."*
> George Bernard Shaw

Yes, we somehow all know that to be true about communication; it is the sender's responsibility. We also know that a lack of communication or bad communication is the source of many relationship and productivity problems. So, even though we know this, the communication process at times still breaks down. More accurately, we experience a breakdown in the communication process with someone, the sender or the receiver.

With communication problems, either the sender or the receiver is unfamiliar with the successful communication-cycle model (and, as such, just needs to be educated in the communication process), or either the sender or receiver is incapable of working properly within the successful communication-cycle model. They are negatively influenced by their Primitive Soul.

## *Exercise Break*

Look at all the different people and relationships in your life and let's assess your communication success:

Step 1. Identify how successful you believe your communication is with each relationship in Table 3, rating your success from 0 to 5, where the scores are as follows:

0 — Communication is nonexistent in any form (verbal or non-verbal); you or the other person completely avoids any contact.

1 — Communication is very limited; only when necessary is there any interaction, and the interactions are kept short and to the point.

2 — Communication is formal, limited, and cautious; you communicate only what is necessary, and you stay away from personal or controversial topics.

3 — Communication is casual, yet limited; you communicate what is necessary, and on occasion, you may include personal or controversial topics.

4 — Communication is comfortable and enjoyable; most topics are open for discussion.

5 — Communication is extremely comfortable, almost all topics are open for discussion, and sometimes you even think the other person can read your mind or knows what you are thinking.

Step 2. If your communication success does not score a 4 or 5, identify what you believe is limiting your communication. Are the issues with you or with the other person? Be as specific as you can.

### Table 3. Rating Relationship Communication

| Relationship | Communication | |
|---|---|---|
| | Rating | Limiting Issues |
| Spouse/partner/significant other | | |
| Children | | |
| Parents | | |
| Siblings | | |
| Friends | | |
| Coworkers | | |
| Boss | | |

## Primitive Soul Communication Style

Let us take a look at how Primitive Soul-motivated individuals communicate:

Joan (in the middle of the busy office): Fred! FRED!!!

Fred: WHAT!!! Can't you see I'm busy!

Joan: I don't care. You were supposed to finish the Offshore marketing report this morning. Where is it? I am really tired of repeating myself with you. No matter what I tell you, you NEVER get things done around here. I am SO tired of ALWAYS covering for you. I don't know why this company puts up with your lack of performance. If I was running this place, things would be working a whole lot differently. Am I getting through to you?

Fred: Offshore? I clearly heard you say it was the Onshore marketing report and you made it sound like today was a "nice to have," not a hard deadline. It's not like I have all the time in the world to write YOUR reports. And this morning the traffic getting into work was SO horrible, with two accidents on the freeway and then the parking lot was backed up for blocks....

Joan: Your commuting troubles are not my problem, and I clearly told you that the Offshore marketing report was due this morning, not "sometime"...

Samantha: Joan!

Joan: WHAT! Can't you see I am talking!?

Samantha: Well, too bad. Bob needs to see you RIGHT NOW with that Offshore marketing report!

Joan: You tell Bob I'll be there when I am ready!!!

This is the communication and conversation style of three Primitive Soul-motivated individuals all trying to get their way, with no interest in or empathy for the others. Joan, Fred, and Samantha are all in it for themselves, and their communication style is the result of that. The others in their world are merely there for their convenience.

The key component necessary for successful communication is for the sender and the receiver to have a high degree of empathy[21] for each other. For the sender to ensure that the message is received correctly, he or she has to have some degree of empathy for the receiver. Without empathy, the sender cannot inquire of the receiver to discover the degree of accuracy and completeness of the received message.

---

21 Empathy — the sense and ability to understand another person's feelings, thoughts, and emotions.

Primitive Soul-motivated people have a lot of inherent problems communicating successfully and having decent conversations because empathy is challenging for them. Because life is all about them, Primitive Soul-motivated people expect everyone to know what they are thinking and feeling (when it's convenient for them); it's a "can't you read my mind?" kind of attitude.

> *"Wise men speak because they have something to say; Fools because they have to say something."*
> Plato

Following is the viewpoint of Primitive Soul-motivated people in regard to communication and conversation:

- They are not interested in your stories, just their stories, and to emphasize the importance of their stories, they use drama and exaggeration — they never let the facts get in the way of a good story.
- They do not like being interrupted. What they need to say is far more important than what you are saying, so they will interrupt you.
- They expect you to be listening just because they are talking.
- They are more about solving your problems than listening to them.
- They choose to forget what they said so they do not have to apologize for what they said.
- They need to get in the last word.

## Angelic Soul Communication Style

Now let us see Joan, Fred, and Samantha a little differently, same office, same three people, but with an Angelic Soul motivation this time:

Joan: Fred, there you are!

Fred: Hey! Good morning, Joan. Did you find the Offshore marketing report on your desk this morning?

Joan: Yes, I sure did! And it is exactly like what we talked about on Monday afternoon. And I want to thank you SO MUCH for helping me out of this jam; I owe you one. You were such a great help and I appreciate all the time you put into it.

Fred: I don't mind giving you a hand. I know you were under a big time constraint.

Samantha: Hi, Fred.

Fred: Hi, Samantha.

Samantha: Joan! Whenever you are ready, Bob will meet with you to discuss the Offshore marketing report.

Joan: Yes, thank you. Please tell Bob I have what he needs, thanks to all of Fred's help, and I will be in his office in ten minutes.

As compared to the previous version of this conversation, this is a wholly different event. This is the communication and conversation style of three Angelic Soul-motivated individuals all working together to accomplish their needs, the needs of others, and the needs of the group (or the company, in this case). They are all supportive and have time to accommodate each other's needs. This is a different conversation, with different results, driven from an Angelic Soul perspective. Angelic Souls understand that proper communication is their responsibility.

For the Angelic Soul-motivated person, good communications and conversations come naturally because the Angelic Soul has empathy for other souls since they are driven to be in relationships. Following is the viewpoint of Angelic Soul-motivated people in regard to communication and conversation:

- They are great listeners, focused on others' needs in addition to their own.
- They have concern for another's well-being.

- They understand everyone has the need to be heard.
- In conversation, they know everyone has the need to preserve their identity, and they see the uniqueness in each person.
- They take responsibility for their parts of the conversation.

## Mixed Soul Communication

Assuming we cannot avoid communicating with Primitive Soul-motivated people forever, we are going to have to do our best to make it successful. Remember, they are communication challenged. So, you need to communicate on their schedule and on their terms; attempting to do otherwise may result in conflict, hurt feelings, yelling and screaming, finger pointing, and guilt trips. When communicating with Primitive Soul-motivated people, whether as the sender or receiver be aware of what is going to occur during the conversation. There are specific communication obstacles to look out for and to be prepared for:

- They will dominate the conversation by talking over others or telling grand stories; Primitive Soul-motivated people have a hard time being just a receiver.
- They will talk down to you, because you cannot be trusted or are incapable of understanding the message.
- They will use tricks to get their way in the conversation — using drama, speaking loudly, exaggerating the facts, playing the martyr, and laying the guilt trip.
- They will need to be right and if the conversation is not going their way they will simply change the subject to avoid the issue.

When in conversation with Primitive Soul-motivated people, to improve the communication cycle, we need to:

- Understand the situation, do not overreact, relax, and have patience with their communication style.
- As the sender in the communication cycle trying to get your message across, talk to their "all about me" motivation, which includes giving them credit and recognition for their contributions.

- As the receiver in the communication cycle trying to understand their message, understand that they think you are untrustworthy and incompetent to understand their message, or that you are a convenient ear to hear their story.
- Do all you can to stay with your Angelic Soul.
- Stay with the successful communication-cycle model.
- Ignore the drama, exaggeration, and the guilt trip; listen for the important pieces of information.
- Do not take what they say personally, especially the guilt trip — it is not about you.
- Let them have the last word.

Good communication skills are essential to success in life because life's successes and happiness usually involve others. Most important to good communication — or, second on the list after speaking the same language — is empathy, or the ability to perceive another person's message. It allows us to stay focused on the sender's true message instead of trying to think of a better story or what we want to say next or interrupt with our "better" story. With a lack of empathy, Primitive Soul-motivated people cannot project themselves into someone else's circumstances, so they cannot understand another's problems, life, or message, because they are focused on their own life or story. Good communication and conversation is about having a true relationship between sender and receiver.

> *"Everyone wants to be heard, but nobody wants to listen."*

## Key Takeaways

1. The objective of real communication and conversation is the successful back-and-forth exchange of messages (information or ideas) between two or more people, the sender and the receiver.
2. The sender needs to ensure that the message was received correctly, accurately, and completely.

3. The key component of successful communication and conversation is empathy (the sender and receiver being able to relate to one another).

4. Primitive Soul-motivated people are troubled communicators. They have inherent challenges practicing empathy because life is all about them.

5. Angelic Soul-motivated people are good communicators. They naturally have empathy because they are driven to be in relationships with other souls.

6. When communicating with Primitive Soul-motivated people we need to:
   - Understand the situation, do not overreact, relax, and have patience with their communication style.
   - Give them credit and recognition for their contributions.
   - Understand that they think you are untrustworthy and incompetent to understand their message or that you are a convenient ear to hear their story.
   - Do all you can to stay with your Angelic Soul.
   - Stay with the successful communication-cycle model.
   - Ignore the drama, exaggeration, and the guilt trip; listen for the important pieces of information.
   - Do not take what they say personally, especially the guilt trip — it is not about you.
   - Let them have the last word.

# CHAPTER 11

# FEELINGS AND EMOTIONS

*No emotional crisis is wholly the product of outward circumstances.
These may precipitate it. But what turns an objective situation into a
subjectively critical one is the interpretation the individual puts upon
it—the meaning it had in his emotional economy; the way it affects
his self-image.*
— Bonardo Overstreet, Understanding Fear in
Ourselves and Others

FEELINGS ARE A VERY TOUCHY subject for human beings. They rock us to our core. Feelings somehow affect our very identity. Dealing with feelings means facing the reality of which soul we spend the most time in. Emotions are the outward display of inner feelings, the part we all get to see and experience.

Feelings and emotions are responses and reactions to events occurring in the world around us. They can manifest both mentally and physically — for example, laughter, crying, tears, pain, smiling, frowning, and stress. When we believe events in the real world result in something favorable or pleasing to us, we respond or react with "positive" feelings and emotions,[22] such as desire, happiness, hope, love, lust, or passion. When we believe the events of the real world

---

22 Positive feelings and emotions — the ones that make us feel good about ourselves and life and that bring good energy to our life.

result in something unfavorable or displeasing, we respond or react with "negative" feelings and emotions,[23] such as loneliness, anger, feeling dejected, despair, discontent, disgrace, dissatisfaction, envy, fear, hate, feeling isolated, jealousy, feeling overwhelmed, pity, sadness, shame, sorrow. Basically, when we are:

> *"Negative emotions like loneliness, envy, and guilt have an important role to play in a happy life; they're big, flashing signs that something needs to change."*
> Gretchen Rubin

- Happy and excited, life is going our way
- Angry and upset, life is not going our way

Feelings and emotions are transitory; they come and they go. We can be happy one moment, sad another. Usually, negative feelings and emotions seem to last longer than the positive ones. Feelings and emotions can be a type of stimulus-response — you get poked, you cry until the pain goes away.

In contrast to the transitory nature of feelings and emotions, a "state of being" is a much more stable emotional place or achieved emotional level. Positive states of being are bliss, contentment, delight, ecstasy, happiness, joy, love, and peace; negative states of being are grief, misery, sorrow, sadness, suffering, and unhappiness.

The degree or severity of our emotional response is based on a combination of conditions:

- Our current state of being
- The magnitude of our response or reaction to a specific outside event or circumstance

Let us say, as an example, you are in a *happy* state of being and something good happens to you (a happy event) — so now you become even happier. From the outside, your new level of happy might not look that much happier, because you are still in a happy state of being (see Figure 15). However, when you are in a *sad* state of being and the same happy event happens, you become happy. From

---

23 Negative feelings and emotions — the ones that make us feel bad about ourselves and life and that bring bad energy to our life.

the outside, this happy event may move you from your sad state of being to a happy emotional state (even if it is a temporary state of being) (see Figure 15). Of course, the opposite might be true if an unhappy event was to occur.

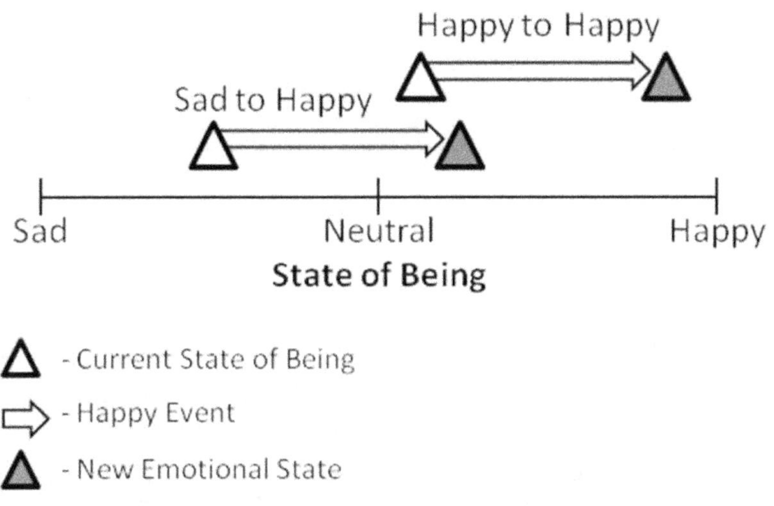


**Figure 15. Transitory emotional states.**

The more we live out of our Primitive Soul, the more we are affected and driven by our feelings and emotions (see Figure 16). This is because of the influence of all the Primitive Soul motivational factors: Abundance and Prosperity, Pain and Pleasure, and Identity and Belonging. All of these body-based "I need it now" motivating factors constantly push us to seek instant mental and physical gratification, or what feels good right now. So, to measure our success in achieving the goals of the Primitive Soul, we need constant feedback from the real world. This constant real-world feedback produces a lot of up and down feelings and emotions.

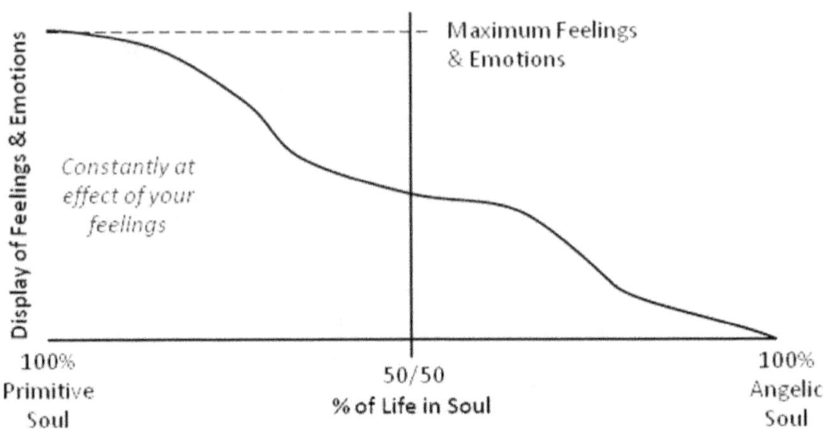


**Figure 16. Those affected by feelings and emotions.**

Primitive Soul-motivated people express wins and losses in life with big up-and-down displays of emotions. The bigger the win or loss, the bigger the up or down in the display of emotion. The Primitive Soul drives us on an emotional rollercoaster (see Figure 17).

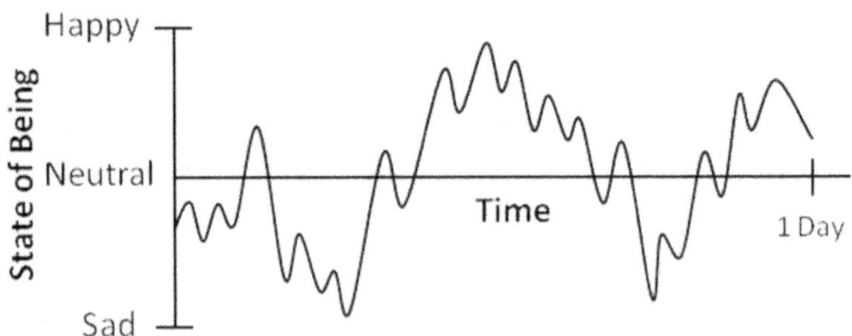


**Figure 17. Primitive Soul emotional rollercoaster.**

When we live more out of our Angelic Soul, we achieve a stable state of being. The Angelic Soul does not require constant feedback from the real world. It knows there is a future; it understands about being in it for the long-term; and it is not as motivated by temporary wins or losses as the Primitive Soul is (see Figure 18). The Angelic Soul can ride out many of life's bumps.

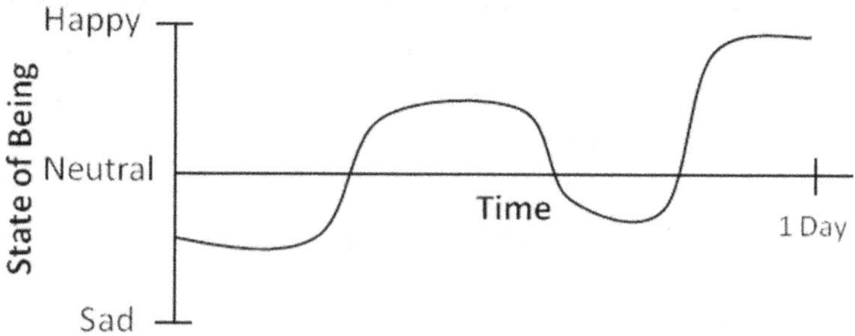

**Figure 18. Angelic Soul emotional rolling hills.**

Emotions and feelings are responses to situations and the environment. These responses are based on our current state of being and, most importantly, the soul we are operating from at the moment. Of the negative emotions, anger and guilt are the ones that need to be specifically addressed because of their major effects on our health, relationships, and success. We will address anger now and guilt gets its own chapter.

# Anger

If you have ever been angry at someone for something they said or did (or did not say or do), then this is for you — being angry is all about YOU; it is personal. Our anger has little to do with what the other person said or did because *they* said or did whatever it was. Someone else might have responded with "Oh well" and moved on, but instead, their actions evoked anger in you. Anger arises when real life does not match up with our imaginary world or the way we think life should be according to the scenarios that play out in our head. In certain situations, some specific mismatch with our expectations

> *"Speak when you are angry and you will make the best speech you'll ever regret."*
> Laurence J. Peter

triggers us to respond with anger, so that makes our anger our own responsibility. Anger immediately moves us into our Primitive Soul (if we are not already there), and as such, all that we do and say while we are angry comes from being in our Primitive Soul. Be careful what you do and say while you are angry because its effects can continue well beyond present time.

## Pain and Injury

Pain and injury, though not emotions or feelings, do have emotions and feelings associated with them, and can also very quickly move us back into our Primitive Soul. Again, be careful what you do and say in a state of pain — legitimate or not, what you say or do may be very hurtful to others around you.

On the other hand, when you are present to someone who has been injured, is in pain, or is angry, be very aware that they are in a Primitive Soul-response mode. When a person is in Primitive Soul-response mode, we need to:

- Be aware of the situation and do not overreact.
- Know whatever they say and do it is most likely *not about us* and we are not to be blamed (at cause) for the situation.
- Move to our Angelic Soul and comfort them from there.

## *Key Takeaways*

1. The degree or level of feelings and emotions is based on a combination of our response or reaction to a specific outside event or circumstance and our current state of being.
2. When living out of our Primitive Soul side, we are more affected and driven by our feelings and emotions. We experience a constant need for instant mental and physical gratification. This constant real-world feedback produces a lot of ups and downs in feelings and emotions; it's an emotional rollercoaster.

3.  When living out of our Angelic Soul side, we are in a more stable state of being. The Angelic Soul, aware that there is a future, does not require constant feedback from the real world; it understands about being in it for the long-term and is not as affected by temporary wins or setbacks.

4.  Anger is personal. Look to yourself to calm the anger and do not blame others.

5.  When a person is in Primitive Soul-response mode, we need to:
    - Be aware of the situation and do not overreact.
    - Know whatever they say and do it is most likely *not about us* and we are not to be blamed (at cause) for the situation.
    - Move to our Angelic Soul and comfort them from there.

# CHAPTER 12

# GUILT FEELINGS

*I think guilt is directional. You should get rid of it, but the way to get rid of it is not to get rid of the guilt feelings. It is to get rid of the wrong that you did that caused the guilt feelings.*
— Philip Yancey, Christian author

POPULAR BELIEF IS THAT GUILT is an unfortunate side effect of being overly exposed to either social norms or religious morality. Some people even believe that guilt is a special right and privilege of every mother to inflict upon her children or that it is the exclusive tool of religious or ethnic groups to control their members' behavior. Whatever the source, guilt is most certainly a negative feeling — maybe the worst feeling in the world.

> *"Food, love, career, and mothers, the four major guilt groups."*
> Cathy Guisewite

It could eat you alive. It could destroy you. Why? Because guilt is the worst form of mental pain — it plays directly to the Primitive Soul's motivation to avoid pain — and we cannot leave guilt behind; it lingers in our past and continues to haunt us in the present. We fear guilt because it is often painful to confront and deal with. We usually will do just about anything to reduce the pain of existing guilt feelings and to avoid any future guilt-creating situation or person.

## Guilt Mechanism

Guilt works like this: it washes over us right after we come to realize that we (may) have done something wrong. Guilt is the feedback we get from the Self-Regulating Human Behavior subsystem within the internal Human Operating System. This subsystem acts as built-in checks and balances. Guilt feelings are the feedback that indicates that we have done something "wrong." There are five parts to the guilt mechanism (see Figure 19):

> *"Now, I don't want to get off on a rant here, but guilt is simply God's way of letting you know that you're having too good a time."*
> Dennis Miller

1) The action we "did" [24]
2) How the action is deemed "wrong"
3) The trigger that forces us to look at the action
4) The resulting guilt feelings
5) How we respond to the guilt feelings

---

24 Did — includes all that you did, said, felt, or thought or did not do, say, feel, or think or something you should have done, said, felt, or thought or should not have done, said, felt, or thought.

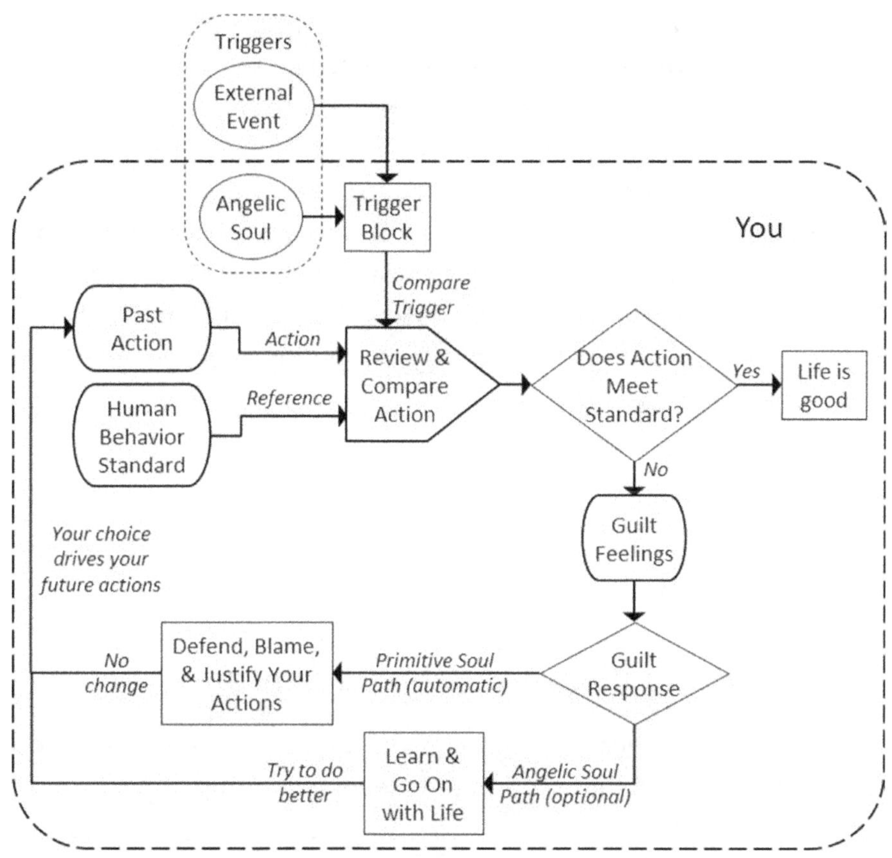


**Figure 19. Guilt response mechanism of the Self-Regulating Human Behavior subsystem.**

## Our Guilt-Bearing Actions

The action we did "wrong" could be just about anything we "did" in the past; what is most critical about the action is that it is an action we cannot go back to change, fix, undo, or alter its outcome. We did an act that is unalterable — this is called the guilt-bearing action. Guilt-bearing actions can range in severity from seemingly trivial acts to grave errors:

- We did not hold the door for someone whose hands were full.

- We told a lie.
- We hurt someone physically or emotionally.
- We got into a fight with someone we care about.
- We did not say "I love you" to someone we never saw again.
- We cheated on our spouse or significant other.

What is common with all these guilt-bearing actions is that they result from the negative influence of our Primitive Soul; the result of lacking connection with other souls and overindulgent behaviors. We somehow did not take the appropriate action — proper soul flow — in these situations.

## Exercise Break

Identify key guilt-bearing actions in your life. Identify the actions that you feel guilty about. Make a list of these guilt issues.

## Compared to the Standard

How is it that these actions are "wrong"? And who decided that they are wrong? For some action to be deemed wrong, it needs to be compared against some standard, some reference behavior. In the case of guilt, we compare our actions against some human behavior standard. Therefore, for an action to be deemed wrong, it must be contrary to or inconsistent with the objectives and motivations of a human behavior standard. We create our human behavior standard in two ways:

> "I'm just going to say it: I'm pro-guilt. Guilt is good. Guilt helps us stay on track because it's about our behavior. It occurs when we compare something we've done—or failed to do—with our personal values."
> Brene Brown

1) We gather standards from various sources in our environment.

2) We recognize behavior standards that come straight from our Angelic Soul.

Starting from birth, we are exposed to many sources of human behavior standards. Our first behavior standards come from our parents, most likely from our mother. How many times have you done something and the first voice you hear in your head is your mother's, scolding you for what you have just done? Oh, the guilt feelings that brings up!

Then as we grow older and interact more with the wider world, we start to accept and take on the behavior standards of the people and groups around us, and most certainly the ones our Primitive Soul identifies with. These are the behavior standards dictated by society, political and social groups, and religions, the ones that tell us how to believe or act in certain situations. With these dictates also come the penalties for failure to comply. These are the norms, morals, and behavior standards that we learn to accept and identify with, the ones we beat ourselves up over when we fail to comply because we know we could have or should have done things differently.

The problem with these civil laws, social/political norms, and religious standards of morality is that they vary from group to group, sometimes significantly. There is not one set of universal human-generated behavior standards, and this fact leads to conflicts between groups, fighting over who has the proper and right standard of standards.

But what is universally true is that when we live from our Angelic Soul, we always know and do the right actions because that is the way of the Angelic Soul. The Angelic Soul does not take sides. The Angelic Soul is all about being in relationships with other human beings, other living creatures, and things; therefore, the Angelic Soul sets the ultimate human behavior standard.

## Guilt Triggers

You "did" what you "did," and what you "did" is a potential guilt-bearing action. So, when do the guilt[25] feelings happen? Guilt is triggered either the moment our Angelic Soul checks in and makes us realize we did something "wrong" or sometime (days, weeks, years) later when an external event triggers the memory of the guilt-bearing action (see Figure 19). External guilt triggers can come from just about anywhere and anyone — we see or hear something that triggers our guilt mechanism. Generally, external guilt triggers are innocuous and unintentional everyday events, yet they relate to something in our past, mean something to us, and trigger guilt feelings. The act of our Angelic Soul (our internal trigger) or some external trigger forcing us to remember, face, and examine a past guilt-bearing action is the "guilt trip."[26]

## Trigger Block

There is one limitation to the guilt trigger mechanism — the trigger block (see Figure 19). If a person is overly Primitive Soul-motivated — too far to the left on the scale in Figure 20 — the Self-Regulating Human Behavior subsystem remains dormant — untriggered. The deeper a person is into their Primitive Soul motivations — more left on the scale, the less guilt they deal with because they are not motivated by guilt or guilt feelings — the "all about me" Primitive Soul does not care about others and what they think, say, or feel (no empathy), and their Angelic Soul is totally disconnected, unable to make their Primitive Soul aware of its overindulgent behavior.

---

25  Guilt — a negative feeling in response to something your Primitive Soul motivated you to do (or not do), say (or not say), feel (or not feel), or think (or not think) in the past that is contrary to your human-behavior standard.

26  Guilt trip — the path you take in your head after your Angelic Soul or some external trigger reminds you of some past guilt-bearing event.

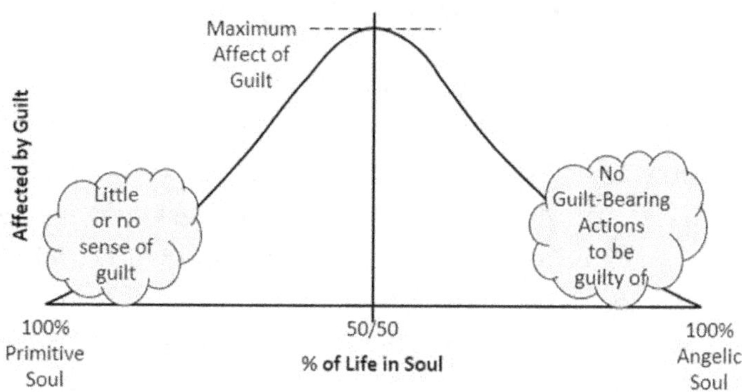


**Figure 20. Who is potentially affected by guilt?**

## Guilt Feelings

The moment after the triggered guilt-bearing action is realized and we regret what we did, the resulting guilt feelings come over us. Similar to anger, guilt in any form is really all about us. First and foremost, as with any feeling, it cannot exist without us giving it permission to exist. And as with all feelings and emotions, the degree of the guilt feelings is based on our current inner state of being. But most importantly, the degree of the guilt feelings is based on the severity of the guilt-bearing action; the more severe the action, the more severe the guilt feelings.

## Guilt Response

After an internal or external trigger forces us to remember and review a past guilt-bearing action and we are suffering the associated guilt feelings, we then respond or react to those guilt feelings. There are two guilt response options: those on the Primitive Soul path or those on the Angelic Soul path (see Figure 19) — there are options of which path to follow only if we know we have the ability to choose; otherwise, we automatically take the Primitive Soul path.

## Primitive Soul Response

On the (default) Primitive Soul-response path, the automatic response to the guilt feelings is to defend and justify our "wrong" actions. We try to explain to ourselves and everyone else why we did what we did and how it is not our fault. Mistakes are *never* our fault; there are always circumstances and people who can be blamed or at cause for our behavior. Therefore, Primitive Soul-motivated people do not learn from the negative results of their actions; it is not their mistake — it is always someone or something else's fault. We rationalize our actions so we can reduce, avoid, or deflect the pain of being wrong for what we did, and this leads us to the end of the guilt trip.

## Angelic Soul Response

On the Angelic Soul path, the guilt feelings can be used as a positive motivator if we allow our Angelic Soul to drive our response to whatever we "did wrong." The response is simple — we accept the mistakes in our behavior and learn from them. We take responsibility for our behavior, grow as a person, and move on, knowing and willing that we will do better next time. In some situations, guilt can do some potential good by forcing us to confront issues and stay on the "right" track. Because we are not perfect, the guilt-bearing action can act as a learning experience on how to be a better person. It can be used to build relationships, not tear them down, and to become a better person when we first take responsibility for our mistakes.

## Guilt - the Great Motivator

Sometimes people deliver an external guilt trigger intentionally; they know what they are doing and why they are doing it. Why do we intentionally induce a guilt trip on someone else?

For all the wrong reasons, guilt is an effective motivator because it is such a strong negative feeling; making guilt a powerful but foul tool to use, especially on the unsuspecting. Guilt can get people to do just about anything. Motivating people with guilt is nasty and manipulative. Nevertheless, guilt as a tool has been used successfully in sales, politics, religion, and parenting.

An intentionally induced guilt trip is a path we take someone down when we want to:

- make them feel bad for something they "did";
- get them to do something for us they probably do not want to do;
- make them feel sorry for us when we want or need something from them;
- get them to leave us alone; or
- deflect the pain of others giving us a hard time — we simply turn the guilt back on them.

The intentionally induced guilt trip can be displayed or acted out in many ways, such as with drama, sarcasm, feeling sorry, worrying, shame, martyrdom, obligation, comparison, or exaggeration. It could sound something like this:

- "I should not have eaten that. Now I feel bad."
- "You just don't understand what a hard life I have" (and all other forms of "life is hard").
- "You're not being fair" and "Life is not fair to me."
- "You do not understand me" or "You are not listening to me."
- "You owe me" (and all other ways of imposing a sense of obligation).
- "Why are you not like your sister (or brother)?"
- "She gave $1,000 to the charity. What are you going to give?"

...and one of the worst guilt trips:

- "You hurt my feelings."

Intentionally induced guilt is a tool Primitive Soul-motivated people frequently use to motivate others. Though these people themselves are unmotivated by guilt, they certainly know how to use guilt as a tool to motivate others. These people are masters at inducing guilt. Since "it is all about them," they have little concern for another's feelings, except to use those feelings against the person. Intentionally inducing guilt in a person is a vicious and cruel form of exploiting another's vulnerability. This induces mental pain. What does this say about the guilt inducer as a person? We use induced guilt because it works (on most people), but it is not a positive form of motivation, and it takes its toll not only on the person receiving the guilt trip but ultimately on the relationship between the two people.

Primitive Soul-motivated people also induce guilt on others as a defense mechanism — someone says something they do not like, so they fight back by laying a guilt trip, such as by saying, "You hurt my feelings." Invoking *feelings* or *drama* is a protection mechanism of the Primitive Soul, and it should alert others who deal with this person that a guilt trip is coming.

When we operate deep within our Angelic Soul — far to the right on the scale in Figure 20, we are not motivated by guilt. There are no Primitive Soul overindulgent behaviors to feel guilty about. And the Angelic Soul, being a relationship-motivated soul, would never consider using guilt as a motivating or defensive tool. Our Angelic Soul knows it would be too harmful to our relationships.

## Guilty as Charged

To avoid or reduce the pain of the guilt trip and to overcome guilt from past guilt-bearing actions, we must first take responsibility for those actions and their consequences. Taking responsibility immediately stops the guilt feelings before they can become overly hurtful. Then we must look at both the action and the behavior standard we have connected to the guilt-bearing actions.

With the behavior standard, determine its source — society, political or social group, or religion — and decide if that behavior standard is still valid for your future life. You need to clean out unsupportive behavior standards. With the guilt-bearing action, in retrospect, review the action and imagine how you will behave differently in a future event if similar circumstances were to occur and how you could have your Angelic Soul present at the time.

We are less controlled by guilt when there are fewer guilt-bearing actions from our past to deal with. The bottom line is: reduce the number of future guilt-bearing actions. We must take the necessary steps to allow our Angelic Soul more control in our life — soul flow. If something

> *"With integrity, you have nothing to fear, since you have nothing to hide. With integrity, you will do the right thing, so you will have no guilt."*
> Zig Ziglar

needs to be done, do it for the right reasons, not out of guilt, and not if it will make you feel guilty in the future.

## Key Takeaways

1. Guilt feelings are the feedback that indicates we "did" something "wrong."
2. Guilt is the worst form of mental pain, and it plays directly to the Primitive Soul's drive to avoid any form of pain, and we will do just about anything to reduce the pain of existing guilt feelings and to avoid any future guilt-creating circumstances.
3. Guilt comes over us right after we realize that we (may) have done something wrong.
4. There are five parts to the guilt mechanism:
   1) The action we "did" — The guilt-bearing action is an unalterable act.
   2) How the action is deemed "wrong" — An action is deemed wrong when it is contrary to or inconsistent with the objectives and motivations of our human behavior standard.
   3) The trigger that forces us to look at the action — Guilt feelings are triggered by our Angelic Soul or by an external event of the memory of a guilt-bearing action.
   4) The resulting guilt feelings — The degree of the guilt feelings is based on the severity of the guilt-bearing action.

5) How we respond to the guilt feelings — We have two choices on how we can respond to guilt feelings:
   o Primitive Soul (default) path: Mistakes are "never" our fault, so we blame circumstances and people for our behavior, we justify or explain why we did what we did and how it is not our fault.
   o Angelic Soul path: We accept our mistakes, take responsibility for our behavior, grow as a person, and move on, knowing and willing that we will do better in the future.
5. Our Angelic Soul sets the ultimate human behavior standard.
6. Guilt is an effective motivator, but it is not a positive form of motivation. It takes a toll on the person receiving the guilt trip and on the relationship.
7. The Angelic Soul would never consider using guilt as a motivating or defensive tool.
8. Guilt can be a potentially good motivator when we use it internally. It can force us to face issues and keep us on the "right" track.
9. We are less controlled by guilt when there are fewer guilt-bearing actions from our past to deal with; reduce the number of future guilt-bearing actions.

# CHAPTER 13

# GIVE AND TAKE

*Rings and jewels are not gifts, but apologies for gifts.*
*The only gift is a portion of thyself. Thou must bleed for*
*me. Therefore the poet brings his poem; the shepherd,*
*his lamb; the farmer, corn; the miner, a stone; the*
*painter, his picture; the girl, a handkerchief of her*
*own sewing.*
— Ralph Waldo Emerson

GIVE A LITTLE, TAKE A little — the whole idea of give and take is wrapped around an exchange cycle, the Give and Take Exchange Cycle. Two parties make up the Give and Take Exchange Cycle, the giver (or sharer) and the taker (or receiver); the object they exchange is the gift (see Figure 21). The Give and Take Exchange Cycle must balance. For someone to give there must be someone to take, and if there is someone who needs, there must be someone who provides. The Give and Take Exchange Cycle includes the exchange of any object as the gift: gratitude, birthday presents, a smile, a handshake, a kiss, a helping hand, a hug, time, effort, money, or even a thought or an idea.

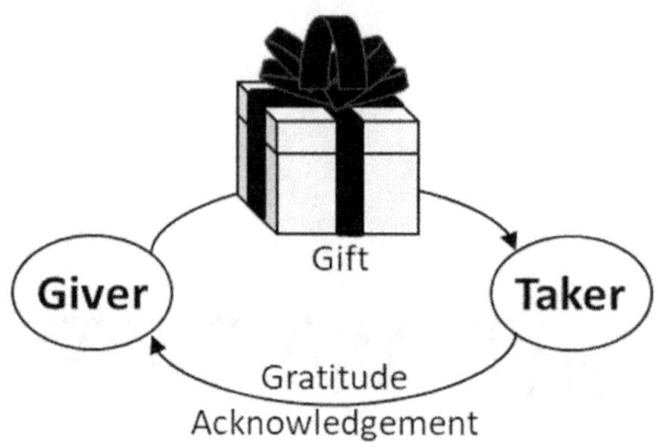


**Figure 21. True and meaningful exchange in the Give and Take Exchange Cycle.**

The Give and Take Exchange Cycle occurs every day, all day. Buying a car, deciding where to eat a meal with your coworkers or spouse, negotiating a contract, giving a birthday present, or holding the door open for someone — these are all examples of the Give and Take Exchange Cycle. There are trivial Give and Take Exchange Cycles, and then there are true and meaningful Give and Take Exchange Cycles. Five criteria are necessary for a true and meaningful exchange:

1) The gift is given willingly by the giver (or sharer).
2) The gift is important, significant, meaningful, or valuable to the giver.
3) The taker (or receiver) honors the giver by taking (or receiving) the gift with gratitude (whether or not the gift has value to the taker).
4) The gift is doubly special if the giver gives a gift that is also important, significant, meaningful, or valuable to the taker.
5) The giver expects no consideration in return for the gift.

The gift must be given willingly by the giver. This is important because if the gift is taken or extorted from the giver, it is not given but stolen and the giver is not a willing participant in the Give and

Take Exchange Cycle. Sometimes giving a gift is necessary and obligatory, but the gift still can be given willingly.

Second, the gift must somehow be important, significant, meaningful, or valuable to the giver. If the gift has no value, then it may be considered worthless, and the taker is only a convenient place to discard the object. Sometimes, though, one person's trash is another person's treasure; just ask a poor, homeless, or needy person. So an object that may have had value to the giver in the past, but no longer does in the present, may have value to the taker, and if the giver truly understands this, then the gift still has value.

Third, the taker honors the giver by taking (or receiving) the gift with gratitude, whether or not the gift has value to the taker. This is when the actual exchange occurs and is completed. The gift is only really accepted when the taker expresses gratitude for it, such as by saying "thank you" or any other words or actions to show acceptance. Without this display of acceptance, the giver does not know whether the gift was received or just taken. This becomes a problem for gifts given anonymously; the giver usually must assume the gift was received by its intended taker and therefore the giver was honored for it.

Fourth, the gift is doubly special if it is also important, significant, meaningful, or valuable to the taker. If the giver takes the time and energy to think about the gift to be given and chooses one that is appropriate to the taker, then the gift becomes extra special because now it is valuable to both the giver and taker, and this makes both parties of the exchange happy to be part of

> *"The excellence of a gift lies in its appropriateness rather than in its value."*
> Charles Dudley Warner

the exchange. If the giver wishes to make a significant impact on the taker, in choosing the gift, the giver should consider the taker's needs and desires.

Fifth, the giver expects no consideration in return. A true gift is one given when the giver does not expect any reward, reciprocity, or consideration in return. This is true giving because the giver knows the giving of the gift was the right and necessary thing to do and gave it willingly, and therefore nothing else is needed in return. The giver does not measure the value of the relationship by any future gift or consideration in return for the original gift. There is no keeping track or score of gift equality or quantity. Each gift is given independent of any past or future gift-giving opportunity, and there is no expectation of recognition or reward, no hidden agenda, only the reward of knowing you are doing the right thing by giving.

Now let us look at how the Primitive Soul and the Angelic Soul each participate in the Give and Take Exchange Cycle.

## The Giving Soul

When two or more people are in a true and meaningful relationship, there is a sense of harmony and connection. This connection makes the Give and Take Exchange Cycle work smoothly, with complete synchronicity, and this level of connection can only occur between Angelic Soul-motivated human beings.

On the front end of the Give and Take Exchange Cycle, there is the giving. There are two ways to give: with an expectation of return and with no expectation of return. The behavior of giving and sharing with no expectation of return exemplifies the "serve the greater good" attitude of the Angelic Soul-motivated individual. We exhibit this selfless behavior with caring, good and righteous deeds,

> *"Giving money is a very good criterion, in a way, of a person's mental health. Generous people are rarely mentally ill people."*
> Dr. Karl Menninger

giving back to the community, volunteering, and putting others' needs before ours (when it is appropriate). Angelic Soul-motivated individuals go out of their way to give.

When Angelic Soul-motivated individuals are on the receiving end of a gift, they accept the gift with humility, almost to the point of making the giver feel that they are undeserving of receiving the gift. This, unfortunately, gives the giver the feeling that the gift is unappreciated and that the Angelic Soul taker is not showing gratitude for the gift (violating criterion 3). Angelic Soul-motivated individuals are more comfortable giving gifts than receiving gifts, until they understand criterion 3 (see Table 4).

**Table 4 — Exceptions to the Give and Take Exchange Cycle**

| Someone who... | Too Little | Too Much |
|---|---|---|
| **Gives** | Selfish<br>Keeps it to themselves<br>No charity<br>No Volunteering<br>Gift is not of value | Love — can't absorb it fast enough<br>Trying to make people feel good about you |
| **Takes** | No gratitude<br>Martyr<br>Does not take gift when being offered | Greed<br>Never satisfied<br>Gift-taking black hole |

## The Taking Soul

When one or the other or both parties in the Give and Take Exchange Cycle are exhibiting Primitive Soul motivations, the Give and Take Exchange Cycle becomes corrupted. The level of corruption can be small or large, depending on the individuals. The Primitive Soul-motivated exchange is then very one-sided, more taking than giving or giving too little when more is needed.

When an individual on the take side of the Give and Take Exchange Cycle is motivated by the Primitive Soul, the behavior of taking and receiving is dominated by the "it's all about me" attitude of the Primitive Soul, along with the motivation for Abundance and Prosperity, or having as much as possible. When a Primitive Soul-motivated individual takes, this wanting and needy behavior appears as selfish, privileged, or entitled.

Primitive Soul-motivated people cannot help themselves. Everything in the universe revolves around them in some way or another and whatever they do is better than what everyone else does because they are special. Or, if they are not better, then whatever happens to them is the worst that can happen to anyone — they are martyrs. Their actions are geared toward what is best for them; they do not willingly make personal sacrifices for anyone else. They constantly feel like they are getting short-changed in life, so they believe they *should be* getting all the extra goodies and gifts; they are entitled.

Primitive Soul-motivated individuals have a hard time executing a true and meaningful Give and Take Exchange Cycle. On the "give" side, they may feel resentment for having to give a gift, and the gift may have no true value to them — they grabbed the first thing off the shelf — or to the taker. But two things are for sure: a Primitive Soul-motivated individual will make sure you know how much the gift costs, and they really need to hear how much you appreciate it, even if you do not.

On the "take" side, Primitive Soul-motivated individuals may not show any true gratitude for a gift; perhaps the gift is not good enough, big enough, expensive enough, or they feel like they deserve it anyway. Have you ever watched a child open presents at a birthday party? Compare their response when a gift is not something they want to their response when they open a gift they definitely want. Children respond from their Primitive Soul all the time when they get gifts — "It's not what I wanted!" Then we tell them to "Go tell Aunty 'thank you' for your present!" anyway. This is the behavior of children. This is the behavior of Primitive Soul-motivated individuals on the take side of a Give and Take Exchange Cycle that is not true and meaningful.

## Greed, Control, and Power

The Primitive Soul is motivated by personal achievement and results (a survival mechanism); this is driven by the need for abundance and prosperity. This in no way implies we actually achieve abundance and prosperity when we act from our Primitive Soul (other factors are involved in actually achieving abundance and prosperity); it just means we are driven to pursue it. This drive for abundance and prosperity appears to others as greed.[27] Achieving personal wealth and fame is the motivation of the Primitive Soul, and it does not need to be on the grand scale of kings, tyrants, corporate CEOs, celebrities, or Wall Street investors. It could be as simple as taking credit for someone else's work, speeding up to keep another car from getting in front of you, cheating on your taxes, hoarding or collecting, or buying a house or car you cannot afford because you must have it to prove your worth.

The Primitive Soul is motivated by having more and better things: home, cars, clothes, shoes, children, and many other possessions. It pushes us to keep up with or exceed what our neighbors, friends, and family have. It must be constantly more and better and we cannot be outdone by anyone; the Primitive Soul must outperform everyone. Primitive Soul-motivated people believe in the saying, "He who dies with the most toys wins." They are very competitive. But the problem with this is they acquire stuff for the wrong reasons.

And to fulfill their greed, they need to exert varying degrees of control and power over their environment and people. Their environment and how they interact with it is an expression of their level of control over it; demonstrated by the décor in their home and office, how neat and orderly they keep things, the amount and size of their stuff, or the make, model, and color of their car — these are all indicators of their control over their environment.

In this drive to win the game of acquiring stuff, Primitive Soul-motivated individuals also need to be in control of their relationships, even the one with their spouse or significant other. When we dominate someone, we are imposing control on them and there is no equality in the relationship, no true give and take.

---

27 Greed — the overemphasized pursuit of material things (money, cars, home, and all stuff in general) and the quantity of those things.

Exerting control and power is the most animalistic ways one human being influences fellow human beings. It is the "Do it my way so that way I get what I want regardless of what you want" way. Control and power, purely animalistic, are useful in survival and emergency situations; however, they are not that effective in one-on-one relationships because the overwhelming desire for taking leads to greed and the need for control and power that result in many one-sided Give and Take Exchange Cycles.

## Entitled and Privileged

Societies all over the world recognize the existence of two specific classes of people — the entitled and the privileged. In each case, the class of people is "granted" certain rights or an exclusive set of benefits. The word *granted* is used loosely here because these rights and benefits are considered gifts simply because they are unearned by the recipients. Sometimes these rights and benefits are set aside by law or group rules, and in other cases, these rights and benefits are assumed for themselves by the group because they believe them to be an extension of their existing rights and benefits or based on their status in society. In either case, these rights and benefits are either gifted to the entitled and the privileged or they are taken by the entitled and the privileged (such as when they consider themselves above the law). In reality, there is no difference between the entitled and the privileged — sometimes it is hard to tell them apart — only by the amount of money or possessions the individuals in each class may have (see Figure 22).

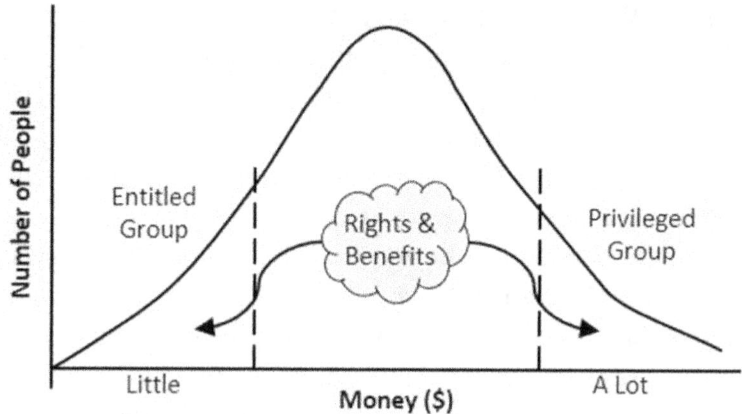


**Figure 22. The entitled and the privileged — two classes of people separated only by money.**

Regardless of what these two groups believe about taking or accepting the gift of the rights and benefits, the problem really lies with the third group — the un-entitled, unprivileged individuals. This is the group that provides the gifts of rights and benefits. It is for this group that the Give and Take Exchange Cycle is being violated:

- First, the gift (assumed to be valuable to the giver) may not be given willingly and, in that case, the rights and benefits are taken, not given (violating criterion 1).
- Second, the takers, the entitled or the privileged, express no gratitude for the gift (violating criterion 3). As a matter of fact, sometimes the takers show signs of contempt for the giver, because they feel they not only deserve the gift but also are owed these rights and benefits.

Whenever we feel entitled or privileged, we violate the Give and Take Exchange Cycle and do not bring balance to it. This results in a major upset for the givers of the rights and benefits.

## Over the Top

You might be wondering, "Can someone help too much, trust too much, give too much, or simply love too much? Because I am always getting hurt." We cannot necessarily give too much because in a Give and Take Exchange Cycle that is true and meaningful, for every gift given there must be a taker who honors the giver by accepting the gift. Remember, a gift can be anything of value, including your heart. The real problem in the idea of giving too much is twofold:

- Giving for the wrong purpose
- Giving to someone who is overly Primitive Soul-motivated

These both violate the Give and Take Exchange Cycle in some way. For example, if we give for the purpose of encouraging or manipulating someone to love us, trust us, or help us, then we violate criterion 5, giving with no expectation of a consideration in return for the gift. In this case, we give with the hope something — love, trust, or help — will be given back; we give with an expectation of a return. This approach to giving will fail almost every time (unless the taker is a solidly Angelic Soul-motivated individual) because the taker usually will not pick up on our hidden agenda and will return nothing. We will almost always walk away from the gift exchange empty-handed.

In such situations, it pays to be honest in admitting that we are giving for the wrong reasons and there will be no true and meaningful exchange, so we are opening ourselves up to hurt. We must be sure not to cover up our intentions of an expectation of a return on the gift with the pretense that we have a good heart and that is why we give so much; we would be fooling ourselves. With love, we cannot keep giving, that is, forcing, it on someone in the hope that they will love us back or that it solves any of our problems with love and relationships.

To be in healthy relationships[28] involves many daily Give and Take Exchange Cycles. When we are in a relationship with an overly Primitive Soul-motivated individual, we will hardly ever achieve balance in the Give and Take Exchange Cycle. With the exchange cycle out of balance, gift exchanges with Primitive Soul-motivated

---

28 Healthy relationships — one in which both parties gain benefit from the relationship.

individuals always lean in their favor. The giver feels (and rightly so) that they give and give and never get anything in return — feedback, acceptance, or appreciation, violating criterion 3. Overly Primitive Soul-motivated individuals are gift-giving black holes — they always take and give little of what is needed in the relationship and the gift exchange. We need to be cautious of these questionable Give and Take Exchange Cycles.

In relationships with Primitive Soul-motivated individuals, we are compelled to give more and more in the hope that someday we will get a positive response or acceptance of our gifts, which in itself violates criterion 5 of the Give and Take Exchange Cycle and so taints exchanges from the start. What we must realize is that the Primitive Soul black hole cannot be filled by what we are providing. We need to stop trying to fill the void in the Primitive Soul; either accept them for who they are or reduce future opportunities for Give and Take Exchange Cycles.

## The Greatest Gifts

The greatest gifts we can give another in a true and meaningful Give and Take Exchange Cycle are those that come from us as individuals — something of ourselves, something no one else can give:

- Our smile — showing the warmth of our heart
- Our love — the love a parent gives a child, one spouse gives the other, or one person gives another
- Our time — the most valuable commodity we each have; it is irreplaceable
- Our skills — the craft of our own hands or thoughts
- Our gratitude — showing our connection with other Souls
- Our patience — taking time to understand another
- A loving, caring act of kindness
- A "please" and "thank you"
- A compliment or words of encouragement

- A hug — one of the best forms of human contact and soul connection

Only Angelic Soul-motivated individuals can dig down into themselves and come up with the right gift to give to the right person at the right time. Our value as human beings is not based on the quantity or monetary value of the gifts we give. Rather, it is based on the depth of our gift giving, the value of the gifts to us and to the people receiving them.

## Exercise Break

Make a list of all the significant people, organizations, and groups in your life. Then add to the list gifts that would be important, significant, or valuable to each. This list can be ever evolving, growing, and changing as your life around these people, organizations, and groups grows and changes, and the gifts that are important, significant, or valuable to them change. Your Angelic Soul should support these people, organizations, and groups.

## Key Takeaways

1. The guidelines for a true and meaningful Give and Take Exchange Cycle are as follows:
   1) The gift is given willingly by the giver.
   2) The gift is important, significant, meaningful, or valuable to the giver.
   3) The taker honors the giver by receiving the gift with gratitude (whether or not the gift has value to the taker).
   4) The gift is doubly special if the giver gives a gift that is also important, significant, meaningful, or valuable to the taker.
   5) The giver expects no consideration in return for the gift.
2. Angelic Soul-motivated individuals are more comfortable giving gifts than receiving them. They must learn to show more acceptance and gratitude for the gifts that come their way.

Remember, taking or receiving a gift with gratitude honors the giver.

3. Primitive Soul-motivated individuals are more interested in taking or receiving gifts than in giving or sharing of themselves, resulting in a one-sided Give and Take Exchange Cycle. Primitive Soul-motivated individuals must learn to be more willing to give of themselves. Otherwise, the overwhelming desire for taking leads to greed and the need for control and power; they take more than they need and are never satisfied.

4. The entitled and the privileged are two groups of people who take gifts that are not given willingly.

5. The real problem with the idea of "giving too much" is twofold:
   - Giving for the wrong purpose, such as giving to force or encourage someone to love you, trust you, or help you in return
   - Giving to someone who is overly Primitive Soul motivated because the Primitive Soul black hole cannot be filled by what you are providing

6. True giving and taking is performed by Angelic Soul-motivated individuals, and it is performed with love. A true giver gives with no expectation of reward. And a true taker honors the giver with gratitude.

7. The greatest gift you can give someone is something of yourself.

# CHAPTER 14

# RELATIONSHIPS AND TRUST

*It takes time and deeds, and this involves trust, it involves making ourselves vulnerable to each other, to strip ourselves naked, to become sitting ducks for each other—and if one of the ducks is shamming, then the sincere duck will pay in pain—but the deceitful duck, I feel, will be the loser.*
— Eldridge Cleaver, Soul on Ice

NO PERSON IS AN ISLAND. Most need to belong to a group and to be in relationships, relationships of all kinds. Some people have a difficult time being without human contact; others can take it or leave it — they might find other people too difficult to understand and deal with. But for most of us, relationships are crucial, useful, and desired. Successful relationships allow us to be productive and happy.

We can be in relationships with just about anyone, anywhere, anytime. However, this book does not address relationships with inanimate objects, animals, or dead people, but with other living human beings. We can have all kinds of relationships in life. Some are casual — people you meet on the street, fellow workers on the job, people you meet at club events, classmates at school, and so on. Some relationships are significant and useful — parents, spouses, children, friends, coworkers — and some of these are determined, meaning we do not choose the individual we are in the relationship with, such as parents, siblings, children, and coworkers. Regardless of how relationships come about, important relationships must be developed in order to flourish and become true, meaningful, and functional. Here we focus on one-on-one relationships, but these principles can apply to relationships with groups and organizations.

A true, meaningful, and functional relationship is one in which both parties grow and gain long-term benefits of some kind. The relationship benefits can be physical, emotional, intellectual, financial, or some combination thereof. Not all of our relationships need to be true, meaningful, and functional; some can remain casual, where long-term benefits do not exist or are not that important. However, the several important and key relationships in our lives — the ones that really count — must evolve into true, meaningful, and functional relationships.

If creating, building, and achieving true, meaningful, and functional relationships were easy, we would be doing it all day long! Why stop with the short list? Anyone we meet could become our future BFF (best friend forever). However, the development of true, meaningful, and functional relationships is not easy because our Primitive Soul motivations interfere with accomplishing that.

To successfully develop true, meaningful, and functional relationships there is a progression of key stages our relationships need to progress through to achieve that goal: first comes connection, then trust, and finally intimacy (see Figure 23). These stages, when successfully achieved, enable us to create these lasting and meaningful relationships.

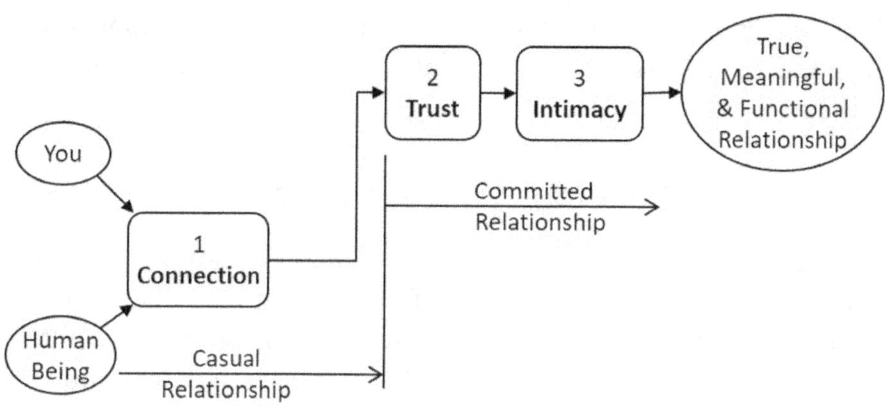


**Figure 23. Stages of building successful human relationships** — from a casual relationship to a committed relationship.

## Relationship Stage 1: Connection

Stage 1 — two people meet, they usually meet over some common interest. But this does not preclude the (very romantic) chance meeting (at a bus stop on a cold and rainy night) or being in the right place at the right time kind of thing. However, for a relationship to continue we need to have a reason to continue it; we need a connection, or a common cause, common interest, or common ground.

The initial connection could be based on similar interests, work, school, activities (gym, clubs, etc.), hobbies, social groups, habits, religious practices, or many other things. It could be made in person or online. The connection could occur one time or be ongoing; you run into this person on a regular basis. It could be based on an intellectual, emotional, physical, or financial interest. This is the start of the casual relationship, and a casual relationship may continue strictly on the basis of the strength of the connection.

If the connection is not strong, the casual relationship is short-lived or very superficial. What determines the strength of the connection are the quantity and quality of common interests between the two parties to the relationship and the degree of importance of those common interests. Also, the stronger the overall connection, the greater the possibility the casual relationship could continue on to the next stage.

## Relationship Stage 2: Trust

Stage 2, the trust stage, is a big step in a relationship. It is the gateway to a true, meaningful, and functional relationship. It is the must-do step to transition a casual relationship into a committed relationship (see Figure 23). Complete trust, to borrow from the American court system, is "the truth, the whole truth, and nothing but the truth." Trust equates to honest, dependable, reliable, and faithful behavior, as in we do and say the right things at the right time in the key areas of the relationship:

- Communication and conversation
- Feelings and emotions
- Give and take

The trust stage is the most important stage of relationships. Without achieving this stage *successfully*, the transition to a true, meaningful, and functional relationship will not occur (more on trust is coming up). When we give our trust to someone, it implies the relationship has become a committed relationship. All true, meaningful, and functional relationships are based on and then built on trust. If a relationship fails to move through the trust stage or if trust is broken or not maintained, the relationship will stagnate or fail.

## Relationship Stage 3: Intimacy

When trust is achieved and maintained throughout the relationship, the relationship transitions quite naturally to stage 3, intimacy. Intimacy means connecting at a soul level, where both individuals' Primitive Souls and Angelic Souls are involved and both individuals' needs and motivations are fulfilled. Intimacy involves knowing someone else's interests and looking out for their interests.

Intimacy implies that two people enjoy being together and that they enjoy high levels of affinity, openness, and closeness. Intimacy means different things in different types of relationships (see Table 5). Not every relationship needs to have the same depth of trust or intimacy; the depth of trust and the level of intimacy relate to the type of relationship we create and how successful we are at building each stage of the relationship.

### Table 5. Intimacy in Different Relationships.

| Type of Relationship | Version of Intimacy |
|---|---|
| Parents/In-laws | Honesty, spending time together, talking about important topics |
| Children | Honesty, spending time together, talking about important topics |
| Family | Honesty, spending time together, talking about important topics |
| Coworker/Boss/Team | Left alone to get job done, involved in company strategy, involved in bigger projects and decisions |
| Friends/BFF | Keeping secrets and sharing secret thoughts |
| Spouse*/Lover | Keeping secrets, sharing secret thoughts, and sex |

* Or some similar arrangement

In relationships, if we skip straight to intimacy too quickly, we run a huge risk of things blowing up and someone getting really hurt[29]:

- Having sex with someone after one or a few dates thinking this is the one and then getting dumped.
- Telling someone, you thought you knew, a big secret about you and then finding it spread all over the internet or the office.
- You told your boss what you really thought of the project and he found you a new department to work in.

---

29 Hurt — being hurt physically or emotionally pushes us into our Primitive Soul and then we will be responding to circumstances from there.

Having an established committed relationship is crucial when people share any level of intimacy, and the key to having a successful committed relationship is the successful continuation of trust.

## *Exercise Break*

Take some time to evaluate your committed relationships using Table 6. List your relationships by individual names, and then evaluate each relationship for connection, trust, and intimacy. Also consider how the other person might perceive your relationship. This evaluation should help you understand where each relationship stands. Expand the list to accommodate all of your committed relationships. This list, too, will evolve and change as your committed relationships change and grow.

### Table 6. Grading Your Committed Relationships

| Relationships | Relationship - Building Stages | | |
| --- | --- | --- | --- |
| | 1<br>Connection | 2<br>Trust | 3<br>Intimacy |
| Parents/In-laws | | | |
| Children | | | |
| Family | | | |
| Coworker/Boss/Team | | | |
| Friends/BFF | | | |
| Spouse*/Lover | | | |

* Or some similar arrangement

## Connection:

1 — Share no interests of any kind

2 — Share few important interests

3 — Share some important interests

4 — Share most important interests

5 — Share almost all or all important interests

Trust (criteria vary based on the relationship):
1 — Cannot trust this person at all
2 — Still testing my trust level with this person
3 — Share only what is necessary with this person
4 — Share most things with this person, but keep important issues private
5 — There are no secrets from this person; they know all my important thoughts
Intimacy (criteria vary based on the relationship):
1 — Not at all comfortable
2 — A little bit comfortable and participate in occasional intimate moments
3 — Somewhat comfortable and participate in some intimate moments
4 — Mostly comfortable and participate in some intimate moments
5 — Extremely comfortable and participate in many intimate moments

## Trust Factor

Trust requires a leap of faith, taking the chance that the trust we have in someone will be both reciprocated — they will trust us — and respected — they will not do anything to jeopardize our trust. Developing trust is the stage where most people mess up in their relationships, where casual relationships fail to move forward or committed relationships fail to be achieved or maintained. This is also where communication between relationship partners breaks down, where feelings and emotions tend to run rampant[30] with one or both parties, where any selfishness or one-sidedness in the relationship starts to accelerate and personal issues are prioritized as more important than the connection.

Being in successful relationships with others requires understanding how the Primitive Soul and the Angelic Soul help and hinder the building and maintaining of relationships. The key understanding is how the Primitive Soul and the Angelic Soul perceive and deal with trust. Trust is not a complicated subject but a deep subject, because it opens many levels of vulnerability. What

---

30 Run rampant — people get angry at each other for saying improper things about them or the relationship, someone gets jealous about what one person has or how someone else looks, and many of the other negative feelings and emotions.

makes trust appear complicated are the various interpretations of it we have developed.

The Primitive Soul and the Angelic Soul determine how trust is applied in any relationship. Each soul sees trust differently. Primitive Soul people say, "You must earn my trust," and trust becomes an elusive target. This approach to trust starts with the assumption "I do not trust you, even if there is no previous evidence not to trust you." Angelic Soul people say, "You have my trust until you violate it." This approach to trust demonstrates an unverified faith in people's trustworthiness; sometimes these people are caught trusting the wrong people.

These two approaches align directly with the Primitive Soul and the Angelic Soul characteristics (see Appendix A). The Primitive Soul at first is untrusting, and its trust must be earned (however, rarely achieving this goal); Primitive Soul-motivated people are skeptical of others' motives. The Angelic Soul right off assumes trust on the basis of its motivation to connect with all souls, and only if someone betrays this trust is it lost. These perspectives are generally how each soul perceives the world in larger terms.

Because the Angelic Soul assumes trust, it often skips right over the trust stage and jumps straight into intimacy (see Figure 24). This is why Angelic Soul-motivated people seem to "get hurt" in relationships — because of their premature faith and trust in others. On the other hand, Primitive Soul-motivated people never quite successfully achieve trust in stage 2 of relationship building, and they continuously struggle with gaining intimacy. Primitive Soul-motivated people believe others cannot be trusted, so they never want to be all-in, a prerequisite to intimacy. In addition, Primitive Soul-motivated people cannot be trusted to perform the other major tasks that support a true, meaningful, and functional relationship:

- Communication and conversation
- Feelings and emotions
- Give and take

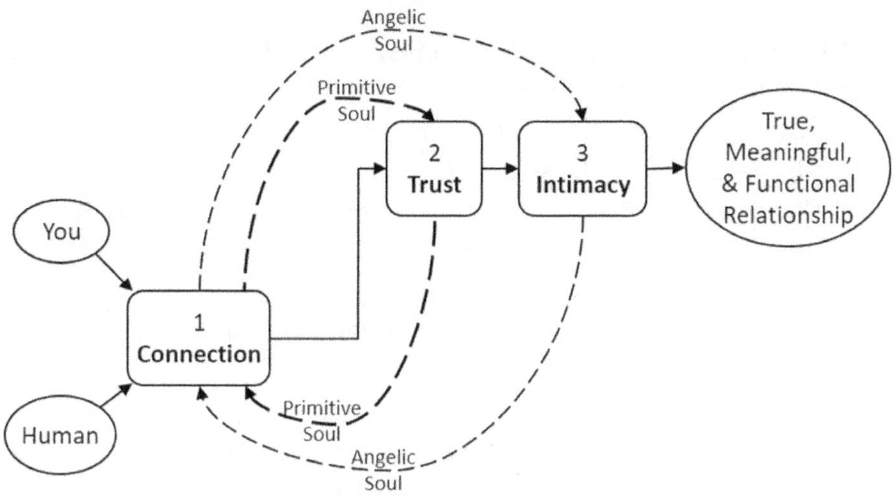


**Figure 24. Souls' unproductive influence on relationships.**

Being in a relationship means a lot of give and take; we cannot always have it our way — that is selfish. In a relationship, we are responsible for more than just our own happiness. The choices we make affect others; otherwise, why be in the relationship?

The key to being in relationships with other human beings is understanding how our own Primitive Soul and Angelic Soul interact with others'. We need to understand our Primitive Soul and Angelic Soul, and then we stand a chance of understanding another's Primitive Soul and Angelic Soul. This challenge is worth the effort, because being in successful relationships returns great rewards — productivity and happiness.

## *Key Takeaways*

1. Successful relationships allow us to be productive and happy.
2. A true, meaningful, and functional relationship is one in which both parties grow and gain long-term benefits of some kind. The

benefits can be physical, emotional, intellectual, financial, or some combination thereof.

3. There are three stages in developing successful true, meaningful, and functional relationships:
   - Stage 1: Connection. A relationship initially created on similar interests — work, school, activities, hobbies, social groups, habits, religious practice, or something else — and established based on intellectual, emotional, physical, or financial interests.
   - Stage 2: Trust. Each party in the relationship behaves honestly, dependably, reliably, and faithfully; they do and say the right things at the right time in the key areas of the relationship.
   - Stage 3: Intimacy. The relationship partners connect at the soul level, and both individuals' needs and motivations are fulfilled at the appropriate levels. Each party knows the other's interests and looks out for their interests.

4. The strength of the connection is determined by the quantity and quality of common interests between two people and the degree of importance of those common interests to both parties.

5. Trust is the most important stage in developing committed relationships. Without achieving trust successfully, the transition to a true, meaningful, and functional relationship will not occur.

6. To have intimacy in committed relationships, trust must first be created and then maintained.

7. Trust requires a leap of faith, taking the chance that the trust we place in someone else will be both reciprocated and respected.

8. The Primitive Soul starts off as untrusting and others must earn its trust. The Angelic Soul starts off assuming trust and trust is lost if others break it.

9. Understanding how the Primitive Soul and the Angelic Soul of each person interact in a relationship is the challenge. It is worth the effort because being in relationships returns the great rewards of productivity and happiness.

# CHAPTER 15

# FREE WILL, FREE CHOICE, AND SELF-CONTROL

*God, our genes, our environment, or some stupid programmer keying
in code at an ancient terminal—there's no way free will can ever exist
if we as individuals are the result of some external cause.*
— Orson Scott Card, American novelist

HUMAN BEINGS ARE UNDER THIS grand illusion that we have free will
and free choice. We have this great belief in our apparent ability to
exercise free will and free choice. Free will and free choice are factors
that most people believe set human beings apart from the animals.
All other fauna and flora follow strict patterns and principles in their
daily lives and activities. We humans insist on having free will and
free choice because we believe it contributes to our need to be in
control of our lives and our environment.

Important note: free will and free choice should not be confused
with the Primitive Soul motivation of self-gratification — doing

whatever it wants, whenever it wants to. They are distinctly different (details to follow).

The idea of free will and free choice is that we have the ability to make decisions and take appropriate[31] actions at the appropriate time and place, based on the current situation, circumstances, or events, independent[32] of predisposed motivations or restricted ways of choosing or acting. What free will and free choice are *not* are habits, routines, or ruts, or any conditioned actions or responses we perform unconsciously or automatically. This is not to insinuate that *all* habits or unconscious actions are bad. Not at all; the act of going to the gym every other day could be a good habit. The routine of hanging out at the bar with coworkers until two o'clock in the morning is most probably a bad habit[33]. But what is really bad is when we are in a rut and keep making the same mistakes over and over again, and then wonder why all these bad things keep happening to us. If we really have free will and free choice, we should be able to do things we do not normally do, regardless of whether it violates some personal rule, habit, routine, or personal identity characteristic, so that we can realize better outcomes.

There are a variety of thoughts and ideas about free will and free choice over a spectrum of beliefs, spread across many cultures, religions, and peoples:

- Some people believe our lives are completely preordained (some would say we are like a puppet at the end of a string) by an all-mighty being or spirit or our fate is implanted in our DNA, unchangeable.
- Some people believe we are dealt a set of circumstances at birth and in life and then we have to find our own way from there, and whatever happens is by luck and chance.

---

31 Appropriate — this is the key factor when it comes to free will and free choice.

32 Independent — another key factor when it comes to free will and free choice.

33 Good and bad habits — a habit should be deemed good or bad based on whether it supports the continuation of a healthy body and the motivations of the Angelic Soul.

- Some people believe they have complete free will and at any time are free to choose whatever they want and how to deal with the random events that come up in their lives.
- Some people are not sure which way to believe, and they try to hedge their bet one way or the other.

## Exercise Break

What habits, routines, ruts, or rules do you have (good and bad) that you keep doing without much thinking or consideration? What things do you do because that is the way you have always done them? Here are a few examples to help you create your own list:

- Exercise or doing no exercise
- Starting your day with drinking coffee
- Watching television shows
- Yelling or arguing with someone specific
- Blaming others for your problems
- Never changing your opinion or position on a subject
- Dating or marrying the same type of person each time

Start your list now and keep adding to it as you discover others.

## An Act of God

There is a conflict inherent in the idea that some divine being — God — has some say in our lives. Either our entire life is preordained or predetermined — often called destiny because God knows all and sees all — or we have complete free will and free choice and life is a series of random events we happen upon. Potentially there is a third option: a higher being sets our purpose in life and we have free will in the choices we make to achieve our destiny — we just do not know ahead of time what it is or when and how.

> *"The conundrum of free will and destiny has always kept me dangling."*
> William Shatner

It does seem that situations, circumstances, and events appear randomly in our lives, and these sometimes are attributed to acts of God (by some groups of people). That belief may or may not be true, but regardless it does not change the real-life occurrence of the situations, circumstances, and events.

So, God may put a car accident in your life, but how you react and respond is an opportunity to exercise free will and free choice. God may give you the winning lottery numbers, but how you spend the money or allow it to change your life is an opportunity to exercise free will and free choice. God may offer you a boat to save you from the rising floodwaters, but it is your free will and free choice to accept the offer and get onboard before you drown. There are moments in our lives that seem not to be of our own making. Among these seemingly random moments of chaos, we have a lot of opportunity to exercise our free will and free choice.

## Free Will or No Will

The key word in the phrase "opportunity to exercise our free will and free choice" is *opportunity*. If some people can exercise free will and free choice some of the time, then for the sake of the discussion, we will assume all human beings have the ability to exercise free will and free choice, regardless of whether they actually do. However, along with the assumption that we all have the ability to exercise free will and free choice, we also know that not everyone does exercise free will and free choice when they could. We often miss the *opportunity* to do so.

> *"We must believe in free will, we have no choice."*
> Isaac Bashevis Singer

Whatever your belief in regard to free will and free choice — life is divinely ordained or a series of random events — what will help you in real life is the ability to make decisions and take actions *independent of your predisposed or restricted ways of choosing or acting.* To unlock our ability to exercise free will and free choice, we need to know and understand our predisposed or restricted ways of choosing or acting — our ruts, habits, and routines. What predisposes or restricts our way of choosing and acting is wrapped up within the key characteristics of the Primitive Soul and Angelic Soul (as listed in Appendix A).

We are in charge of our own life, but only to the degree to which we understand and control how our Primitive Soul and Angelic Soul really influence and affect our decision making. The reality is *we have a soul-driven lack of free will and free choice* when our Primitive Soul or Angelic Soul responds automatically to the situations, circumstances, and events of life. Those automatic responses may not be the *appropriate* ones. Here are some possibly inappropriate predisposed or restricted ways of choosing and acting; when you are committed to them, you forfeit the opportunity to exercise free will and free choice:

> *"Free will is an illusion. People always choose the perceived path of greatest pleasure."*
> Scott Adams

- Instant gratification: The need to have everything you want NOW, with no regard for future ramifications. You will not put off the instant benefits because you believe you deserve it for whatever reason.

- Pleasure seeking: Going after those things that bring you the most physical or mental pleasure (you are driven by what "feels good") with little regard to the cost or impact in the long-term to you or to people around you. Seeking pleasure saves you from making the tough decisions and drives you to take the easy way out.

- In it for yourself: All the decisions you make are for your own personal interests. You have little regard for the interests of others around you when

> *"God gave us free will and we may choose to exercise it in ways that end up hurting other people."*
> Francis Collins

deciding what to do; you do not readily sacrifice your rewards or pleasures, and you think little of mentally or physically hurting others.

- Giving in to peer pressure: You are in competition with others, comparing yourself with what others have or do, and keeping up with others drives your purchases and attitude.

- Giving into fears and emotions: You play to your emotions and fears. You have to know how you feel and how something makes you feel to determine the direction you go in. You allow yourself to be influenced by your irrational fears, avoiding certain things because of their perceived danger.

- Being in control: You have strong desires and need everything to be done your way because you know what is right and how it should be done. You must be the leader, not a follower.

- Needing to be right: You cannot lose an argument or make a mistake in public — no way that is going to happen — regardless of whether the facts are on your side. And if you are right, you are going to make sure that someone knows that you are right, and you are going to rub it in.

- Succumbing to a guilt trip: When you are operating out of guilt feelings, you are easily manipulated. You are easily cornered into a position with limited acceptable options. You so much want to avoid the guilt that you try to quickly get out of the uncomfortable feelings of the guilt trip.

- Controlled by your own rules: You live by an unwritten set of life rules — call them your "shoulds" and your "should nots." You created some of these rules and inherited others, but you hardly question whether they are valid for controlling your life.

- Controlled by others' opinions: What certain people or groups think, say, or believe in is important to you; it is part of your identity. And many times you just follow these people and groups without understanding how their beliefs really affect your life or whether they make any sense.

- Self-sacrifice: You have strong desires to make others happy and meet their needs, and you would never consider hurting another. You think of others before you think of yourself, sometimes leaving your needs unfulfilled.

- Living out of the past: Looking too much to the past (your memories and experiences, past successes and failures) leaves you unable to see new opportunities and experiences in the present. You connect and equate the past with the present; therefore, nothing new and no change is possible. You are left with empty hopes, unfulfilled dreams, and the same old, same old.

- Identity protection: When something happens that challenges any of your personal identity characteristics, you respond by defending your identity. You do not see beyond the identity threat, and all facts become irrelevant. The need to protect your identity forces you to do and say all kinds of strange things. *Your identity is probably your greatest limiting factor in exercising free will and free choice.*

## Soul Flow - Maximum Free Will and Free Choice

Most people are under the illusion that they have free will and free choice. But most people are fooling themselves. No one has complete free will and free choice because the following factors keep us from exercising complete free will and free choice:

- Physical limitations: Bodily, environmental, and natural; limitations that we can do very little to change.

- Cultural and civil limitations: Civil and communal laws and rules; limitations that we have some control over but agree to be limited by.

- Most significantly, we have soul-driven limitations (soul-based motivations) — limitations that we have significant control over if we learn how and choose to.

Unless (or until) we gain self-control over our automatic soul responses, we have no free will and free choice, period, end of discussion. We are driven toward fulfilling our Primitive Soul's needs and desires, and most of the time that presents an inappropriate response to situations, circumstances, or events. To maximize our ability to exercise our greatest free will and free choice at any moment, we need to maximize our ability to freely move between our Primitive Soul and our Angelic Soul — we need soul flow. Soul flow[34] allows us to choose the appropriate soul to operate out of at any time.

## Self-Control

Soul flow does not free us of the influences or the motivations of our Primitive Soul or our Angelic Soul. Instead, it frees us to move between the souls, and in that freedom of movement is the freedom of choice, leading to the maximum degree of free will and free choice. Maximum free will and free choice can only occur when we have complete self-control over our soul response.

When someone does not want to take responsibility for their indiscretions or lack of good judgment, they blame their lack of self-control on some outside force, not on their lack of free will and free choice — it's the "The devil made me do it" defense. To have self-control we need to have

- knowledge — of who we are and what our motivations and opinions are;
- honesty — about what we are willing and not willing to do and about how committed we are to hearing other points of view or changing who we are and how we react to life's situations, circumstances, and events;

---

34 Soul flow — the ability to freely move between which soul influences a situation or to choose the appropriate soul to do the appropriate responding to fit the current real-world circumstances.

- openness — to learning new ideas or changing our ways or opinions; and
- responsibility — for our actions and the results of those actions, not blaming others for our lack of results.

Look at free will and free choice like this: lack of free will and free choice is like being in a compact car on a one-lane road — we can only move forward or backward. We are defined (limited) by the road we are on, its direction and its destinations. Or we can be in an open field in an all-terrain vehicle, where we are free to move in any direction depending on where we want to go. In the open field, we have complete freedom to respond (move) appropriately; we have complete free will and free choice.

## *Key Takeaways*

1. Free will and free choice is the ability to make decisions and choices or to take the *appropriate* actions in current situations, circumstances, and events *independent* of predisposed or restricted ways of choosing or acting.
2. Free will and free choice should never be confused with the Primitive Soul's motivation to do whatever it wants, whenever it wants to.
3. Human beings are under the grand illusion that we have free will and free choice.
4. The reality is we have a soul-driven lack of free will and free choice.
5. Our identity is probably the greatest factor limiting our exercise of free will and free choice.
6. Soul flow frees us to move between our Primitive Soul and our Angelic Soul, and in that freedom of movement is the freedom of choice, leading to the maximum degree of free will and free choice.

7.  Maximum free will and free choice can occur only when we have self-control over our soul response. To have self-control means to have
    - knowledge,
    - honesty,
    - openness, and
    - responsibility.
8.  The power of free will and free choice is that it allows us the greatest ability to adapt to new surroundings and people and changing situations, environments, and events.

# CHAPTER 16

# LIVING IN YOUR OWN WORLD

*Face reality as it is, not as it was or as you wish it to be.*
— Jack Welch, former CEO of General Electric

IF YOU HAVE GOTTEN TO this point and you have not had several "ah ha" moments, spiritual revelations, or personal realizations about your human nature and your life, then this chapter is most certainly not only for you but also about you. The human world exists in two parts: the *real* world[35] and the *illusionary* world.[36] And you are most certainly living in your own world — in the illusionary world.

The real world part is simple to understand. It is the world that we wake up in each morning — reality. The real world is present time — the now — and all that is happening in the now (the car in front of you cutting you off, the baby crying in the airplane seat behind you, the good morning kiss from your spouse or lover). The real world is also the past — all that has happened, the history of the world and

---

35 Real world — the world as it actually occurs without any interpretation; the material world in which human beings and everything else exists.

36 Illusionary world — the world we create in our thoughts, driven by the motivations of our Primitive Soul.

your history. The real world includes all that has happened and all that is currently happening.

The illusionary world is a bit more elusive and convoluted. It is a world that we each create to disconnect from the real world. It is the theoretical world that we would like to live in full-time if we could have our way. It is the world in which we have it all:

- More money
- More stuff, toys
- More control of our life
- A different set of parents or family
- A different group of friends
- A better spouse or lover
- A better job or career
- A better body, health, looks, and beauty
- An easier and more grand life
- A world that most certainly revolves around us

How we split our time between living in the real world and living in our illusionary world determines how well we interact with others and make useful and productive decisions. Of course, ideally, we should be living in the real world 100 percent of the time, interacting with others and making decisions on the basis of what is actually occurring and what has factually occurred instead of whatever we think or would like to be happening. The problem with our illusionary world is that it is mostly inconsistent with reality, and because of that any decisions we make based on our fabrications of our illusionary world will lead us further astray from reality or more into conflict with it.

> *"Life is what happens to you while you're busy making other plans."*
> John Lennon

## Exercise Break

Describe the illusionary world you have created in your mind; be as specific as you can and write it all down:

- Who are you?
- What do you have?
- Where do you live?
- What do you look like?
- What do you believe about yourself and the world?

## Life Lived in an Illusion

To some degree or another, we all live some time in our illusionary world, the world we each have created for ourselves. It has a present time component along with a past and a future. However, the illusionary world by definition does not really exist, other than as a construct in our mind. In our illusionary world, facts and truth are irrelevant because we can fabricate any faux reality we want:

- Our *beliefs* become more important than fact, reality, or truth.
- Our *opinions* become more important than fact, reality, or truth.
- Our *version of the truth* becomes more important than fact, reality, or truth.
- Our *interpretations of our experiences* become more important than fact, reality, or truth.

## Not My Fault

In the real world, we are conscious and aware of our actions and opinions. We take responsibility for all our actions, good and bad. If we say something in error, we own up to it and correct our mistake. We do not point fingers of blame at others when things go wrong or when they do not go our way. We admit and acknowledge being wrong or off track and change whatever needs changing so it will not happen again.

In our illusionary world, we do not take responsibility for anything we do wrong. We do not admit to being wrong to anyone or even ourselves because being wrong is not our fault. It is never our fault. Someone else had to have contributed to the problem, and therefore they are to be blamed. Or the circumstances were out of our control. We deflect all blame. We blame what we cannot control; therefore, we are not obligated or required to change it, and neither are we capable of changing it.

## False Pride

In the real world, we are interested in and open to new beliefs, thoughts, and ideas, even if we may not agree with them. We know our beliefs, thoughts, and ideas do not define us; they are not our identity. We understand our opinions are based on interpretations of the facts as they are presented and, as such, they could be open to change. Disagreeing with someone's differing opinions, point of view, ideas, or lifestyle does not violate our beliefs or invalidate them, so we are not threatened by others' beliefs or opinions. We can disagree with something, ignore it, or listen to both sides and discuss the pros and cons of the subject matter.

In our illusionary world, our beliefs and opinions are supremely important, inviolate, and unalterable. No one can change our mind because our beliefs and opinions have become part of our identity — and what affects our identity leaves little to no room for change. What is erroneous about our illusionary world beliefs and opinions is that they may be loosely based on real facts and truths, and this, in turn, leads us to create more beliefs and opinions that support our distorted, made-up view of the world.

Along with how we hold tightly on to our beliefs and opinions, we also respond to others' beliefs and opinions that differ from ours in a limited and entrenched way. We are not open to facts, truth, or differing opinions because having to defend and discuss our fabricated beliefs and opinions leaves us open to criticism that may challenge our identity. Losing an argument means losing credibility and, most importantly, losing our identity. In many cases, our beliefs and opinions are indefensible, so even a logical and unemotional discussion could never win others over to our side. So, we resort to emotion, drama, lies (or half-truths), and exaggerations instead to make our point and somehow be convincing.

But most useful in our arsenal to defend our beliefs and opinions is how we build ourselves up by putting down others for believing in what they believe. We do this by making light of their beliefs with jokes or by taking cheap shots at them personally. We think it is okay to joke about something or someone when we do not agree — this is called being a bully. Ultimately, if all that does not work, we simply change the subject to avoid the issue altogether.

## Rules to Live By

We all have a set of life rules[37] that guide the way we run our lives and that determine the way we make decisions and interact with others. In the real world, we want and need to do things that are appropriate,[38] and to accomplish this, our set of life rules is a small set. Because too many rules create inflexibility and to react appropriately in the real world we need to remain flexible — there is an appropriate time and place for everything. We apply this small set of life rules fairly and equally to ourselves and to others.

In our illusionary world, we have so many life rules that run every part of our lives: how we dress, act, and treat others; about the car we drive, house we live in, job or career we pursue, person we marry, and so on. Some of these life rules are our shoulds and should be's:

- Life *should be* easier.
- I *should* only have to do the minimum to be appreciated.
- You *should* call every day to show you care about me.
- You *should be* concerned about me and my well-being.
- You *should* spend your money on only these certain things.
- You *should be* living life a certain way.

---

37 Life rules — an unwritten (usually unconscious) set of guidelines for life's action and conduct. Many life rules are sourced from religious dogma. Other life rules are self-created from past experiences and adopted teachings from influential individuals.

38 Appropriate — moves you in a forward direction; solves the actual problem at hand.

- You *should* vote for, marry, and spend time with these specific people.

A large subset of these life rules define how we expect others to interact with us. You see, in addition to the multitude of life rules we have established for ourselves, we have another set of life rules and standards for other people and we apply them selectively, not equally or fairly, because they are dual standards. In addition to having a different set of life rules for everyone, we also force our life rules onto everyone, expecting others to live up to our rules and standards, even if they are not aware of them. We do this either to make life easier or harder for ourselves. In either case, we do it so we can be *right* (which, conversely, makes others wrong and can induce guilt feelings). Mostly, we apply these life rules so that we can get away with our own inconsistent behaviors and actions.

## Alternate Realities

In the real world, there is only the real world, the here-and-now. We have a past, but we do not live in it; we learn from it. The past allows us to understand the present and helps bring meaning and purpose to the present. A characteristic of our human nature is our awareness of a future — a tomorrow. We can talk about a future, but the future really never comes; there is only the here-and-now in reality. But our awareness of the future and knowing we will live another day encourages us to plan for tomorrow and not just live for today. Thinking of a future allows for hope and faith, but, most of all, it allows us the time and space to find the purpose and meaning of life in the here-and-now.

Our illusionary world is made up of many time zones, and we operate in some or all of them. These time zones are almost like multiple parallel universes. In addition to the present, the past, and the future, we have the "What Could Be" reality, which is like an improved future if only the present were all different, more to our liking. Then there is the "What Could Have Been" reality, where, if only we had made better or different choices in the past, things would have turned out different.

The problem with all these alternate realities is that we go around life as if they were real, like living a lie, and whenever we tell a lie (such as living in these alternate realities) long enough, we soon start believing it. If we keep acting like our lives were different (though our life did not actually change) we will start acting as if our life were different — nothing changed but our erroneous belief. But because our illusionary world and the real world are not equal, our actions and decisions are strangely inconsistent, even downright wrong, in reality. And because of our Primitive Soul motivation to be right, we try hard to justify our inconsistent decisions and actions in the real world, which leads to very strange results and responses from others.

> *"It is always a relief to believe what is pleasant, but it is more important to believe what is true."*
> Hilaire Belloc,
> *The Silence of the Sea*

## Unique Ways of Looking at Life

In the real world, we see the world as it is, for all its splendor and glory, its beauty and starkness, its simplicity and complexity, its humanity and peace, inhumanity and hate. We do not make light of it, nor do we exaggerate it. We take life as it comes at face value without under- or overinflating it. We can perceive and see things from someone else's perspective, can "walk in their shoes," regardless of whether we agree or disagree with their perspective.

In our illusionary world, we constantly create unique points of view and perspectives on how we see ourselves and others, on how we interact in the real world, and on how we justify our (seemingly irrational) actions and decisions in

> *"It's funny how everybody considers honesty a virtue, yet no one wants to hear the truth."*

the real world. We see ourselves and others from the underlying assumption and belief that we are somehow superior and others are inferior and that nobody is as competent as we are. Unfortunately, we are not honest with ourselves, and others certainly cannot be honest with us, for that would be an attack on the life rules of our illusionary world. In our illusionary world, life has no real meaning and purpose, so we may create false meanings and purposes. We see life as a daily struggle that we do not understand, and we believe this is a one-trick pony, a once-and-done life.

From this perspective, we interact with the real world in the belief that everyone should live like we do and believe like we do, because (we believe) we know what is right. We know what we want and the way we want it to be. We believe everyone should bend to our convenience, that our time is more valuable than anyone else's and that we should not have to go out of our way.

On the flipside, we also believe the world is out to get us one way or another. We justify and rationalize our immoral, illegal, and unethical behavior as if certain laws and rules do not apply to us — we are privileged. So, we will make a left turn when the sign says "right turn only"; we will pilfer office supplies from work, and then we convince ourselves "it is illegal only if I get caught." (And this is why a sign or a law does not stop someone from doing something wrong.)

Right or wrong, consistent or not, we justify our actions and decisions by looking for the right evidence to fit our beliefs or by ignoring or diminishing the facts that do not fit our beliefs and views of the world. We selectively adopt information and interpret experiences. We search for, ignore, or eliminate the facts that do not fit or support our stories, beliefs, or opinions. We rationalize or belittle the facts as unimportant or extraneous if they do not fit our stories, beliefs, or opinions. The stories, scenarios, and interpretations in our head scream louder than the realities of life. And when the real-world truths do not fit our illusionary-world images (stories, scenarios, and interpretations) we tend to selectively exaggerate the lies and the truths to fit our beliefs. In the end, we are so afraid of being wrong that we perpetuate the lies.

## Interactions

Because no person is an island, we must interact with other human beings daily to accomplish tasks or simply to be in relationships with them. Successful interactions are mutually satisfying, meaning both parties to the interaction get something beneficial out of it. To have successful interactions, both parties must be in the real world and operating predominately from their Angelic Soul. The greater the degree to which both parties are operating in the real world and from their Angelic Soul, the greater the likelihood of a successful interaction.

Successful interactions tend to be simple and to the point, with no complex or difficult to understand messages or hidden agendas. They are honest and complete, with no drama, no exaggerations, no lies, no posturing for a superior position, and no pretenses. They are not subject to a litany of misinterpretations or misunderstandings or, most certainly, guilt trips. When something does go wrong with an interaction, one or both of the parties own up to it by taking responsibility for their actions and then fixing whatever went wrong. An Angelic Soul says, "I'm sorry," and "Please forgive me."

> *"When you lack truth, all that's left is exaggeration."*
> Greg Gutfeld

The challenge exists in how to interact with others who are living in their illusionary world when we are either in our illusionary world or in the real world (see Table 7). When either party to an interaction is in their illusionary world, there cannot really be a successful interaction. The illusionary world is elusive and subject to change; it's not the platform for two human beings to share for their interactions. Illusionary world interactions are all interpretations of what happened, not what actually happened. When we are in our illusionary world, we distort the past to fit our Primitive Soul-motivated needs. We mold interactions to fit our needs. We may get angry just because we do not get our way or we might use anger as a way to make a point. The more we are in our illusionary world, the fewer successful interactions we have.

**Table 7. Real World and Illusionary World Interactions**

| | | You are in the... | |
| --- | --- | --- | --- |
| | | **Real World** | **Illusionary World** |
| **Others are in the...** | **Real World** | Highest potential for successful interactions. All needs are considered. Honest and open communication. | Anger. You don't understand why the other person doesn't understand. You'll lay a guilt trip. |
| | **Illusionary World** | Confusion and frustration. You are very careful not to upset them. You deal with drama, guilt, and exaggerations. | Self-satisfaction. Nothing successful happens. No one is being heard. |

When two Primitive Soul-motivated individuals interact, both are trying to be right at the same time. Being right when we are in our Primitive Soul means we are in our illusionary world, with all our own interpretations of the real world. It also means we need to be in control and we cannot trust people. When two individuals get together in an interaction and they both insist on being right at the same time, the interaction is going to be interesting, exciting, and most likely unproductive. The conflict between the two can be violent and upsetting. So, though two wrongs don't make a right, two rights make a fight.

## Truth

Have you looked in a mirror lately and really seen what everyone else sees? Or have you listened to yourself speak and really heard what everyone else hears? We know all the right things to say, but we do not lead by setting the proper example. As good as it may appear to live in our illusionary world; the benefits are outweighed by the costs. Despite what we think to be true of ourselves in our illusionary world, we may appear to others in the real world as egotistical, narcissistic, unapproachable, arrogant, self-centered, aloof, or naïve — and these are just the nice ways to say it.

We all wish for a better, different, or more fulfilling life or world in some way or another. However, more dangerous than just wishing for a better or different life is operating as if we have already obtained it — making decisions and forming opinions. When we do that, we are living a life that is inconsistent with the real world. There is a big difference between life the way it "is" and life the way we would like it "to be."

Truth in our illusionary world is questionable and open to interpretation because it is an elusive subject for our Primitive Soul. Our Primitive Soul filters and interprets real-world facts and truths in our illusionary world. We each learn our own set of truths. Everyone builds their own set of truths.

Just because someone tells us something we want to hear or something that fits into our illusionary world model, that in no way makes it the *real* truth.[39] We can pretend the real truth does not exist, but hiding from the real truth in no way invalidates it. We can fabricate stories to embellish or exaggerate the truth or to hide the facts, but, again, hiding from the real truth in no way invalidates it. There is exaggeration and there is real truth — but the real truth is never an exaggeration and exaggeration is never the real truth.

When someone challenges our illusionary world with real-world facts and logic big enough to disrupt our illusionary world and we cannot counter their argument, we resort to the only defense left to us — deflection. We either change the subject or deflect the discussion with tangential, irrelevant information. When we notice

---

39 Real truth — the unalterable facts of the world, the ones few can argue are not real. It is not what we believed happened, but what actually happened.

this happening, we know the other person is addressing a subject that is very personal and it is a good time for us to evaluate the purpose of the illusions that we have created and to own up to the illusion and to shut down this unnecessary controlling factor in our life so we can start living in the real world.

## Living in an Illusionary World

Because our Angelic Soul's ultimate goal is to seek out a greater purpose for living, to contribute to the universe, to love, and to create long-term prosperity and happiness, and because our Angelic Soul has a fundamental understanding of right and wrong and truth, it has no need to construct an illusionary world to live in. Our Angelic Soul is constantly looking for ways to improve and grow, both individually and within relationships. An illusionary world gets in the way and limits our Angelic Soul from achieving its purpose.

Our illusionary world is purely a fabrication of our Primitive Soul. It is based on imagination and is driven by the "it's all about me" and "what's in it for me?" characteristics of our Primitive Soul. We first create our illusionary world when we are children, and we have never outgrown it — we still wish for someone to save us or fix everything. It is like still believing in Santa Claus, the Easter Bunny, the Tooth Fairy, and knights in shining armor as an adult. Ultimately, the size, depth, and degree of detail of our illusionary world are determined by the following:

- How far out of touch our Angelic Soul is
- The degree to which we dislike or cannot cope with the real world

The reason we live in an illusionary world, the real benefit, is that we get to avoid dealing with the real issue: *ourselves* and the suppression of our Angelic Soul. Our Primitive Soul creates our illusionary world to protect us from

> *"People don't want to hear the truth because they don't want their illusions destroyed."*
> Friedrich Nietzsche

the pains of the real world (i.e., bad relationships, unfulfilled goals, hard work, living up to expectations, and so forth). Our illusionary world is for the sole purposes of making us feel good about ourselves and protecting us from the cruel realities of life:

- That our opinion may not be the truth
- That the world does not revolve around each of us
- That we cannot be right and in control all the time

When we operate under the illusion that we are in control, it looks like we are telling people what to do and how to do it. And if this simple, direct means of control does not work, we revert to indirect control tactics: the use of guilt, drama, exaggeration, and acting like a martyr.[40] We use these indirect control tactics to get people to feel sorry for us, like we are a wounded puppy, and that puts us in control.

The trouble with our illusionary world is this:

- We do not realize or acknowledge that it is only an illusion.
- We are unwilling to hear the truth about our fabricated world.
- We believe our illusionary world is real.

We defend every aspect of our illusionary world because our Primitive Soul aims to protect our identity and opinions. We use just about any means (guilt, drama, exaggeration, outbursts of anger, even violence) to protect our illusionary world. We have to. Otherwise, if someone dismantles even just a small part of the illusion, our whole world may crumble and fall away, leaving us with an unfamiliar and uncomfortable reality — the real individual that we are, the one we have been hiding away, working hard to not confront.

When our Angelic Soul loses influence over our lives, we have a difficult time turning off our illusions and living in the real world. If we want to grow as a person, we must hear the truth about our human nature and our illusionary world. We must come to terms with what works

> *"Above all, you must be honest with yourself."*
> James Dean

and what does not work. Living in our own world, our own reality,

---

40 Martyr — you take one for the cause and in this case it is you. You exhibit this by suffering, because, if you cannot be better than everyone else, you are worse off.

only keeps us from dealing with the real world and ourselves. Our illusionary world is our Primitive Soul corrupting our thoughts. We must question our version of truth and the illusions that comprise our illusionary world. Straight up: we need to live in a world without illusions. We need to live in the real world.

For success and happiness, we need to apply our life rules congruently — the same for ourselves as for others. We do not need to jump out of our illusionary world all at once, but we do need to question it one issue at a time. We need to allow our Angelic Soul more influence over our life. We do not get a "do-over";[41] we only get a "do forward." The more we live in the real world, the more connected we are to the people and things around us. These improved connections lead us to better actions, responses, interactions, and life-changing decisions.

## Key Takeaways

1.  The human world exists in two parts — the real world and the illusionary world:

    The real world is
    - the world that we wake up in each morning and
    - present time and also the past, all that has happened and all that is currently happening.

    The illusionary world is
    - the world we create as a fabrication in our mind, a world that does not really exist and that is disconnected from reality;
    - the theoretical present-time world that we would like to live in if only we could have our way, or the future world that never comes; and
    - a place where facts and truth are irrelevant; our beliefs, opinions, versions of the truth, and interpretations of our

---

41 Do-over — children use this tactic when playing games, when they are losing, as an opportunity to start their turn over again.

experiences are more important than fact, reality, or the real truth.

2. The problem with our illusionary world is that it is mostly inconsistent with reality and, because of that, any of the decisions we make in our illusionary world lead us further astray from reality. Nothing is solved by making decisions based on wishful thinking or life conditions that do not exist — nothing!

3. In the real world, we take responsibility for our actions and change. In our illusionary world, we avoid responsibility for our actions and cast blame.

4. In the real world, we know our beliefs, thoughts, and ideas are not our identity; we are open to change. In our illusionary world, our beliefs and opinions are important, inviolate, and unalterable because they have become part of our identity; no one can change our mind.

5. In the real world, we have a small, flexible set of life rules that guide our way in life and we apply them equally to ourselves and others. In our illusionary world, we have a multitude of life rules that run every aspect of our lives, a list of shoulds and should bes, and we do not apply these life rules equally or fairly to others.

6. In the real world, we have only the real world, the here-and-now; we do not live in the past, but we learn from it. In our illusionary world, we have many made-up worlds we operate in and we go around life as if they were real.

7. In the real world, we see the world as it is and we take life as it comes. In our illusionary world, we constantly create unique points of view and perspectives on how we see ourselves and others.

8. Ideally, we need to be living in the real world 100 percent of the time so that we interact with others and make decisions on the basis of what is actually occurring and what has factually occurred.

# TAKE THE BIG STEP

# CHAPTER 17

# MOVING FORWARD AND TAKING CONTROL OF YOUR LIFE

*Two roads diverged in a wood and I — I took the one less traveled by,*
*and that has made all the difference.*
— Robert Frost

NOW THAT WE HAVE LEARNED all this interesting information about our human nature, we come to the crossroad: the time when we need to deal with the truth. If you are older than, let us say, twenty-four years,[42] it is undeniably time to deal with the truth about yourself and consider that you are predominately a Primitive Soul-motivated individual with some Angelic Soul tendencies. To not start from this perspective is to fool yourself. When you start questioning your Primitive Soul's "all about me" habits and attitudes, you adopt a more accurate and honest perspective on life. If you do not do this, you

---

42 Twenty-four years old — about the age when most children transition (mentally and emotionally) to adulthood.

will miss all the opportunities to change and grow. And remember, everyone else already sees the Primitive Soul "all about me" habits and attitudes you demonstrate, so you are not hiding them from anyone other than yourself.

This is the point in our journey when you need to make a decision and pick between two options:

- Put this book down and knowingly go back to what you were doing, perpetuating the status quo.
- Decide to grow and improve your life by making needed adjustments to your internal Human Operating System, putting changes into action in your life and creating some real growth.

Everyone has room to change and grow some a little and some a lot. By making the necessary adjustments to our internal Human Operating System (within our Human Control System), we can expect the following outcomes:

- Living life in present time: You will recognize when your response is you "living in the past," in some imaginary future, or is appropriate to the circumstances.
- More aware of actual bodily needs: You will learn to ignore your need for immediate gratification and to understand the long-term effects of your actions.
- Better communication and relationships: You will develop improved empathy for other people and become more aware of their needs and desires, therein improving your ability to communicate with them.
- Increased sense of purpose: You will see life beyond your personal identity; you will open up to the greater needs of people and the world and live your life purpose.
- More love and peace in your life: You will better understand and care for other people, giving up the need to be right and in control.

You may, however, be at the point in your life, regardless of your actual age, where you believe "you can't teach an old dog new tricks."

I say, you are not that "old dog"; you can improve your current state of being by adjusting your internal Human Operating System, and taking your life to the next level. Here is how it is going to happen: first, we revisit the internal Human Operating System basics and highlight, address, and clarify a few critical points to get you on the way to being a person who has complete soul flow control.

## Find Your Life's Purpose

Each of our souls drives us in a different direction, with its different purpose and motivations (as discussed in Chapters 7 and 8). Our Primitive Soul does not need to develop a sense of life purpose because its purpose is preprogrammed and the same for everyone — survive and then thrive. That is a very clear and specific purpose, and we act out of that fairly automatically and, in general, successfully.

Our Angelic Soul is different. Its initial purpose is to prompt us to find our unique life purpose, our mission. Knowing our mission in life allows our Angelic Soul to guide us with its motivational factors, overriding our Primitive Soul impulses when necessary.

We need to address our Angelic Soul's sense of purpose. We need to ask ourselves, "Why am I here?" Having a purpose and being on the path to fulfilling that purpose brings us true happiness. Our purpose may evolve as we grow and change, but a true Angelic Soul life purpose is outside of you and greater than you. A true Angelic Soul life purpose is never about you but always about the greater good for family, community, and society. Not to worry — our Primitive Soul will always handle our personal and physical needs and happiness.

Most people do not consciously think about discovering their purpose in life. If we live mostly from our Primitive Soul, we never end up addressing our Angelic Soul's need for a defined life purpose. But to do so is to step onto the path of an Angelic Soul-motivated life.

A life purpose need not be anything lofty — like working to end world hunger. It can be simple, such as being the best parent for your children, being the most dependable employee at work, or being a volunteer to help the needy in your community. And you may have more than one at a time. You will know when you land on a legitimate purpose because its objective will have nothing to do with your needs or desires and it will not benefit you directly, though you will definitely feel good about yourself when you are working toward it. The bottom line: we need an Angelic Soul-quality purpose so that our Angelic Soul can begin to be a bigger influence in our life.

## Get Over Your Identity Issues

Next, you need to come to terms with *who* you are, that is, your identity. To change and grow, we must first become fully aware and understand who we identify as "me." How do you answer the question "Who are you?" Say, "I am __________" (fill in the blank with as many answers as you can think of). Continue your list of personal identity characteristics from Chapter 7.

Now is the time to come to terms with the somewhat cobbled-together array of personal identity characteristics that you call *me*, the identity that was first given to you along with the other characteristics you have picked up on the path of life. This is an opportunity for you to own your identity for the first time.

Our identity is the number one roadblock to change, growth, and moving forward in life. So much of whom our Primitive Soul wants us to think we are is wrapped up in our identity. Most times, our list of personal identity characteristics both defines and empowers us, but it also limits us. And unless we are willing to let go of and change our existing identity, we will never be able to make any necessary and significant changes in life or even create new identities. The thinking "I am who I am" stops us time after time from any real change and growth.

Even if we *need* to change (which we all do), even if we *want* to change (because we all want a "better" life), we are only *able* to change when we get out from behind the mask of our identity.

Identity always holds us back. Our identity is our boundary and our boundary is our identity. And our boundaries limit our free will and free choice. Our boundaries have become our comfort zone.

Our unchanging identity most certainly limits us from discovering our true life's purpose, because our purpose may not be within the current boundaries of our identity. So, along with finding your life's purpose, you need to *rebrand* yourself, create a new you. This new you needs to be someone your children (if you have any) and your parents would be proud of. Or, said differently, how do you want to be remembered after you are gone? What will be your mark on the world? Remember, your Angelic Soul is not motivated by identity, and so your life's purpose should not become your identity. Knowing your true life's purpose, you will not identify yourself as the Masked Crusader Out to Save the World.

## Exercise Break

After first admitting to yourself that you have room to grow and the opportunity to change, the next step requires a willingness to deal with your identity, which involves:

- Discovering all the personal identity characteristics that make up your identity (continue the list of characteristics you started in Chapter 7).
- Actively choosing the personal identity characteristics that contribute to your future success and that empower you (*keep* those for now).
- Modifying any personal identity characteristics that do not work beneficially toward your future (*change* them on the list).
- Selectively and carefully creating new personal identity characteristics as life requires them (*add* them to the list).
- Dropping any personal identity characteristics that don't work for you anymore (*delete* those from your list and your life).

The tough part is getting rid of personal identity characteristics that no longer work for you. It is difficult because you have identified with them for so long that they have become part of who you are. But in reality that is not who you really are but only the identity you have constructed over the years. This exercise offers you the opportunity to change your identity to include other characteristics that work better toward your future. Look for any personal identity characteristics you are not willing to give up yet and make a concerted effort to understand why.

## Get in Sync with Your Soul Time

Today is yesterday's tomorrow that *never* arrived. Funny thing about the future, it never really comes, and the present goes by so quickly. When all is said and done, all we are left with is our past, our memories. We learn to appreciate this the older we get and the more we live from our Angelic Soul. But this in no way means we should dwell in the past or even act from it. This is the game plan: the future is the time for planning; the present is the time for living; and the past is the time for tracking where we came from and how far we have come.

> *"I have realized that the past and future are real illusions, that they exist in the present, which is what there is and all there is."*
> Alan Watts

Here is a myth about time: time heals all wounds. The only thing time is good for is helping us forget the events of the past, but there is no healing in forgetting. The only way to heal the past is to deal with it when issues come up by understanding our guilt-bearing actions and our personal identity characteristics. Though we cannot change events that occurred in the past, we can change the way we look at or interpret them, and that can only happen in the present. So, the only way to heal the past is to grow in the present, and that will give us a new perspective on the past.

## Future

The future is the place in time for planning life, considering what to do, when to do it, and what it could look like. The future is all those "what if" scenarios: what if this happens? what if that happens? In the present, we set in motion certain actions directed toward the future we want, but life still gets in the way of our plans and we need to then adjust.

Careful; we should not live in present time as if it were the future we had planned — that is wishful thinking or wishful living — like continuing to live the lifestyle we cannot afford. We have to be honest with ourselves. How many times has the present looked like the future we storyboarded in our head? The made-up future is never the place to live out of in present time.

## Past

The past is the place in time for comparing what we wanted to happen with what actually did happen. It is where we judge our successes and failures against our present actions, our setbacks, and our accomplishments. The past is the historical record of our lives. We get to take it with us wherever we go.

Because of our past we harbor guilt, shame, and pride and bring them into the present. Guilt and shame — we beat ourselves up because things did not work out the way we envisioned them. Pride — we danced like a peacock when things came out better than we expected. Then there is the guilt trip — we would have done things differently had we only known better. This is where we beat ourselves up about that we should have known better and how stupid we were for making the wrong choices or not saying "I love you" that one last time. This is where we second-guess our past actions, assigning some false meaning to the outcomes. The past is never the place to live out of in present time.

## Present

The present, the here-and-now, is the only time for living. The present is where life happens in real-time, not in our head. If we are mentally dwelling in the past or the future, fretting about something, or wishing life was somehow different, we are not *living* in present time; it is just that simple.

The present is the time for living life as it presents itself. We base our actions on reality, not past successes or failures or ideal future situations that may or may not happen. The here-and-now is the place to live in present time.

## Work Your Soul Flow

One soul is not fundamentally better than the other. To be happy and productive human beings, we need soul flow, the ability to move *consciously and freely* between our Primitive Soul and our Angelic Soul. Soul flow is about finding the appropriate time and appropriate place for each soul to influence our life. Finding the *flexibility*[43] to move between the appropriate soul in time and place is the answer. Flexibility is important to our future successes, and soul flow is important to developing flexibility in

- relationships,
- health, and
- career, job, or business.

Ask yourself, "Which soul do I spend most of my time in?" We all really, really, really need to wake up about this issue. Soul flow is critical to enabling change and growth. Figure 10 (earlier in the book) shows that most people are Primitive Soul dominant because we are not thinking or acting from our Angelic Soul but reacting automatically from our Primitive Soul most of the time. With

---

43 Flexibility is the ease in moving from one position to another without pain or suffering, like rolling with the punches or maneuvering a PT boat compared to a battleship.

automatic responses, we have no flexibility, which means no free will and free choice, and no soul flow.

Excessive Primitive Soul-motivated behavior leads us to poor communication, anger, narcissism, arrogance, accumulation of material stuff, superiority, and a few other not-so-nice outcomes. Our Angelic Soul is always there for us; it is just a matter of giving it permission to be in our lives. We need to give our Angelic Soul the opportunity to influence our lives by finding and defining our purpose and by being aware of our personal identity characteristics.

Life lived with soul flow may create big challenges, but that is where we must live. Life lived with soul flow also creates the greatest of freedoms — free will and free choice — and maximum self-control in life.

## Stop Justifying Your Actions

To grow and change, we need to get over our need to be right all the time. The need to be right all the time is connected to our Primitive Soul identity motivation. Being right all the time means we get in the last word in the conversation, we cannot lose an argument (even if it is not going our way), and we need to show that we know more than anyone else in the room (by outdoing everyone with wit, wisdom, and knowledge of trivia). Being right all the time is when we do not listen when other people speak because we are right and know all we need to know already, so no one can add any additional or better information. The bottom line: no one can win an argument with us if we are right all the time; everyone else has to lose.

> *"Human beings are perhaps never more frightening than when they are convinced beyond doubt that they are right."*
> Sir Laurens van der Post

The need to be right drives us to justify and rationalize our actions when there is no agreement in the conversation or when our actions make no sense to anyone else — when logic fails, emotion takes over. We might even resort to using guilt to deflect the conversation when it is not going our way, or simply change the subject completely.

For the Primitive Soul-motivated person, right and wrong are very personal. But in reality, there are few absolutes, and everyone comes to their own conclusions about what is right and what is wrong; therefore, when we insist on being right, it really is just our opinion.

This behavior can be downright annoying. Just stop doing this. We each need to admit, first to ourselves and then possibly to someone else, when we have done or said something wrong, and then just move on without proving we are right or justifying our actions. When we continue to try to prove that what we said or did is right, our Primitive Soul is digging a deeper hole for us.

On the flip side, in a discussion, argument, or fight, just say, "You know, you're right," to end it, so you both can move on with life and the relationship. Allow your Angelic Soul permission to preserve the relationship over your Primitive Soul's need to be right. We need to be honest with ourselves first before others will be honest with us.

But our integrity[44] is of far greater value than being right. People appreciate integrity (when we admit when we are wrong), and they feel more comfortable around us when we are honest and genuine. When we stop justifying our actions and honestly look at both sides of a conversation, we develop a greater sense of empathy, creating an opportunity for our Angelic Soul to come out and connect with people.

> *"Have the courage to say no. Have the courage to face the truth. Do the right thing because it is right. These are the magic keys to living your life with integrity."*
> W. Clement Stone

---

44 "Integrity is doing the right thing, even when no one is watching." C. S. Lewis.

## Take Responsibility for Your Actions

The last thing you might want to do is to actually take responsibility for your life, but it is really the first thing we each must do. This is your life — own it. If we believe we are the product of our environment, then we may be inclined to blame others for our state of being. However, blaming someone else for the condition of our lives never allows for any positive change or growth.

The other side of not owning our life is that we expect more from others — like our parents, the government, our job, or life in general — than we do from ourselves. And when we do this, we often find the results disappointing. Taking responsibility and owning our lives leads to freedom, freedom of choice and direction in life.

It is now time to grow up and take responsibility for our own life — the bad with the good. Then (and only then) can we craft our life to how we want it to look. When we take responsibility for our life, we also take responsibility for our actions — what we do and say. And that is how we become the master of our fate, no longer a puppet to our Primitive Soul motivations.

## Setting Higher Standards and Goals

In addition to the boundaries and limitations imposed upon our Human Control System (as discussed in Chapter 5), we each need to now establish our own additional, self-defined standards and goals that we want to live up to and achieve. These new standards and goals in turn will create new additional boundaries and limitations of our own choosing.

More and more, year after year, society keeps lowering its standards, claiming they are too hard to achieve. I suggest that higher standards are not too hard to achieve but rather they cut into our Primitive Soul-motivated self-indulgence and entertainment time and into our Primitive Soul's desire for instant gratification.

Higher standards do not have to be easy to obtain or even obtainable, but they need to be useful and supportive. They represent the ultimate goals and targets for us to strive for each day to be a little better, and *maybe* on our last day on this earth we will have achieved them.

Avoiding higher standards by making excuses for our behavior leads us down the wrong path in life. And because other Primitive Soul-dominant people also want a way out when they fail to meet the higher standards, they will go along with our excuses. In fact, each time we knock down a higher standard and it is accepted, we make it easier to keep lowering the standards — and this is a slippery slope. Lowering standards is buying into the lie, trying to get away with a mistake because everyone accepts our excuse. Lowering the standards needs to come to an end now! No more playing to our Primitive Soul's needs. Now is the time to set higher standards for ourselves, challenging our Primitive Soul and making room for our Angelic Soul to flourish.

Here are the Angelic Soul-determined higher standards we can strive to meet on a daily basis:

- Integrity: Doing what we say we will do regardless of who is watching or not watching. It is not what we say and do in public but what we say and do in private that determines our integrity. People with low integrity suspect everyone has low integrity too and therefore inherently cannot be trusted.
- Honesty: Saying the truth regardless of the consequences. We must be honest with ourselves first, and then we can trust others.
- Trustworthy: Being the person everyone can count on all the time for doing what we said we would do and being honest.

## *Exercise Break*

Look to see what new standards or goals you need to set for your life. Look at the areas in your life where you could be stepping it up, where you are avoiding the challenge, where you are taking the easy way out. Write down your list of new life standards and goals. Keep this list close to remind you when you start to slip up. Grow the list and grow the challenge as successes and time go on.

## Observe and Evaluate

Adjusting our internal Human Operating System means to act more from our Angelic Soul. We must remember to be grounded in the goals and objectives of our Angelic Soul. Our Primitive Soul and body give us incredible opportunities to accomplish many things in life; however, we need to limit some of our Primitive Soul desires to allow our Angelic Soul the opportunity to flourish. To accomplish this, we set standards, boundaries, and limitations, ways in which we can care for and maintain both souls daily.

To have these improved standards, boundaries, and limits, we need to establish rules to guide our daily life. Whether we think so or not, we already live by a set of rules that run our life and these rules are generally unwritten and, in most cases, unconscious. Regardless, a proper set of rules establishes standards, boundaries, and limitations that help guide our life in a positive direction.

In many ways organized religions have made attempts at setting higher standards, limiting or guiding behavior with moral codes, laws, and commandments. And from a secular standpoint, governments do the same thing, establishing rules and laws for the population so we all can live together civilly and harmoniously.

The first step in the improvement process is to admit that our internal Human Operating System needs adjusting: we understand that we are not in a place where we can freely respond from the appropriate soul at the appropriate time and that we are still overly influenced by our Primitive Soul. The overall objective in adjusting our internal Human Operating System is to develop soul flow — the ability to encounter any

> *"I used to say, 'I sure hope things will change.' Then, I learned that the only way things are going to change for me is when I changed."*
> Jim Rohn

situation and consciously know the appropriate soul action to take. The end results of adjusting our internal Human Operating System are as follows:

- Improved interpersonal communication
- Decreased drive to satisfy only our personal needs
- Increased empathy for others

These adjustments, which bring more of our Angelic Soul into our life, also lead to better relationships and increased happiness.

## Key Takeaways

1. It is never too late to learn, change, and grow in life, and *now* is the time to improve your life by making some needed adjustments to your internal Human Operating System.

2. By making the necessary adjustments to our internal Human Operating System, we can expect the following outcomes:
   - We live life in present time.
   - We are more aware of our actual bodily needs.
   - We experience better communication and relationships.
   - We feel an increased sense of purpose.
   - We experience more love and peace in life.

3. Without a life purpose, our Angelic Soul does not have the ability to guide us, and therefore we act predominately from our Primitive Soul.

4. A true Angelic Soul purpose is never about us as individuals but always about the greater good, for family, community, and society.

5. Our identity is our number-one roadblock to change, growth, and moving forward in life. We must let go of and change existing identity characteristics that no longer serve us, or our identity will stop us (time after time) from experiencing any real growth.

6. The future is the place in time for planning; the present is the time for living; and the past is the place in time for tracking where we came from and how far we have come.

7.  It is time for us to grow up and take responsibility for our life. This leads to freedom of choice and direction in life when we are no longer a slave to our Primitive Soul.

8.  We must get over our need to be right all the time, which drives us to justify and rationalize our actions. Integrity is of far greater value than being right.

9.  There is an appropriate place and time for each soul to influence our thoughts and behaviors. We need to give our Angelic Soul the opportunity to better influence our life. Soul flow is about freely moving between our Primitive Soul and our Angelic Soul as appropriate.

# CHAPTER 18

# 12 ACTION STEPS FOR TUNING UP YOUR IHOS

*Personal, inner change without a change in circumstances and structures is an idealist illusion, as though man were only a soul and not a body as well.*
— Jürgen Moltmann, theologian

HERE IS A SIMPLE SET of twelve action steps that will start you on your way and help you stay on track to change and growth in your life. These are steps for the care and maintenance of your internal Human Operating System that give you more control over your Primitive Soul and encourage

> *"We can't solve problems by using the same kind of thinking we used when we created them."*
> Albert Einstein

greater access to your Angelic Soul. These are basic actions you can start today:

- I will... Own My Life
- I will... Live Life as If Someone Is Always Watching
- I will... Live Life with a Sense of Reality

- I will... Take Care of My Body
- I will... Simplify My Life
- I will... Challenge Myself
- I will... Express My Sincere Gratitude, Appreciation, and Apology
- I will... Set Aside Some Quiet Time
- I will... Share Something of Myself
- I will... Find, Define, and Act on My Purpose
- I will... Be the Example for Others to Follow
- I will... Count My Blessings

## Take Daily Action

So here we go. Enjoy the second phase of the journey. This is where theory becomes practice.

Most of us proceed through adulthood ignoring or suppressing our Angelic Soul. It takes constant awareness and encouragement for our Angelic Soul to come out. These twelve action steps help bring our Angelic Soul (that still, small voice) into a more influential position in our life.

Remember to pace yourself. Part of implementing these action steps is unlearning, putting aside, or giving up certain habits, structures, identities, paradigms, opinions, and ideas in order to open space to replace them with more supportive approaches and thoughts.

> *"Faith is taking the first step even when you don't see the whole staircase."*
> Martin Luther King, Jr.

## Action Step Guidelines

Here are a few guidelines for implementing the action steps:
- Display the list of twelve action steps in your personal space at your house and at work, anywhere where you can easily and

regularly see them. This will keep them in your awareness and remind you of them all the time.

- Find someone (or more than one person) to be your mentor, coach, or partner in helping and guiding you toward accomplishing the twelve action steps.
- Implement all twelve steps. The steps work together and all must be worked on. Do not pick a favorite and ignore the others or drop one because it is too hard or does not make sense to you.

## Action Step Process

Here is the ongoing process for implementing the twelve action steps (see Figure 25):

Step 1) Want to Change

The first step in this process is crucial. This is the step where you decide that changing and growing is important to you, that the status quo is not good enough. Not the need to change — we all have that *need* — but the real and genuine *want* to change. You should have discovered by now the need to change, but here you need to take the big step of wanting to change. You also may need to revisit this step on occasion, when the going gets tough

> *"We secretly believe that we can change; it's only other people who can't. In reality, they feel the same about you."*
> Deepak Chopra

or the guilt feelings are too strong. Each day you need to (re) commit to change.

Step 2) Incorporate the Twelve Action Steps

Start incorporating the twelve action steps into your life. Here is how to do it:

a) Start with action step 1, and each month add the next action step until you are accomplishing all twelve on a daily basis.

b) You may start action step 12 right away.

c) You may combine any of the twelve action steps and accomplish two or more at a time.

d) You may want to keep a log or journal of the action steps as you implement them. It is important to track your progress. In the future you will look back to see where you have come from, to see progress, and to make sure you do not repeat mistakes as you try new things.

Make an effort every day (somehow and somewhere) to incorporate the twelve action steps and recommit to them every day. These steps are not a luxury but a necessity.

Step 3) Review Actions and Results

When you see daily events are not going the way you want, reflect on your actions and the results. Spontaneously[45] or retrospectively,[46] stand back (in your head), focus on and *honestly* review[47] your daily results and actions:

a) Review how your Angelic Soul is more present in your daily life or how it could have been more present had you responded differently.

b) Step up your game, and keep challenging yourself to respond better and better each day.

Step 4) Reenact Your Actions

For opportunities that your Angelic Soul might have missed, perform an imaginary "do-over." Revisit and rerun the missed events in your head and imagine how you could have responded differently or better to the circumstance, this time with more attention from your Angelic Soul. Alter the outcome in your thoughts so that your newly adopted Angelic Soul actions create better results. Be more Angelic Soul-motivated in these events; let your Angelic Soul freely express. Revisiting and rerunning these events puts you in a different state of being — relaxed and calm. This imaginary do-over is your rehearsal for next time.

---

45 Spontaneously — catching yourself in the moment of your actions is the very best time.

46 Retrospectively — at the end of the day before bedtime.

47 Honestly review — look how you responded and reacted to the circumstances of your life.

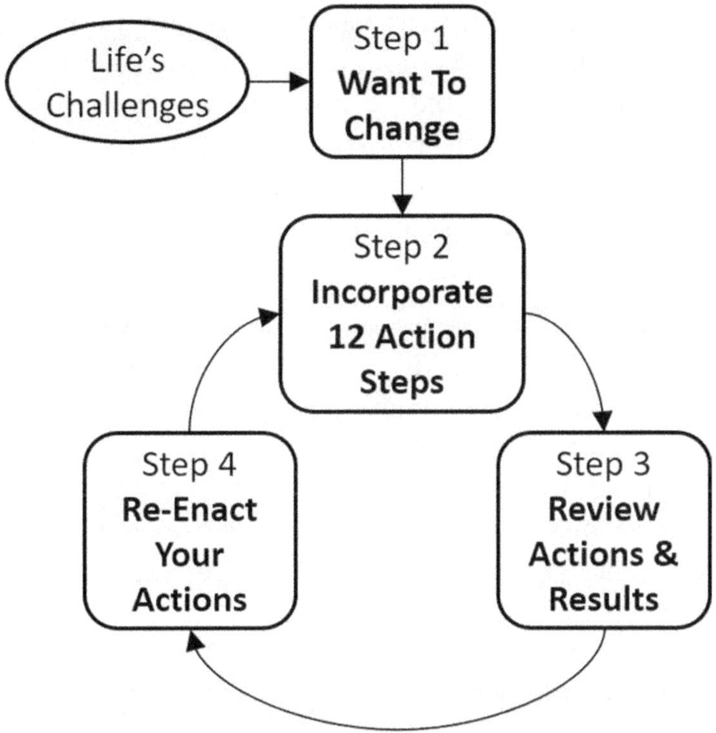


**Figure 25. Implementing the twelve action steps.**
*Follow the process and incorporate all twelve steps into your life.*

Keep executing these process steps (daily, weekly, monthly) as your life improves and then continue executing and repeating these process steps until you have achieved what you want or fulfilled your life purpose.

## Details of the Twelve Action Step

Here are more details to help you understand and implement the twelve action steps:

**Action Step 1: I will... Own My Life**

First and foremost (because without this nothing else matters), say to yourself: If I want my life to change, I will make it happen. I will make the necessary changes to create the "me" I want. People will be there to help, but I must take the steps toward change and growth. No one can want a better life for me more than I do.

In addition to owning the need to change, we must own the consequences and the results by being accountable and responsible. We must accept the bad with the good, and in this way, we own our life. From this day forward, I am the master of my life. I own the life I live.

**Action Step 2: I will... Live Life as If Someone Is Always Watching**

Have you ever noticed that people behave differently when someone with authority is standing there watching? People obey traffic laws when they see a police car on the road. You must from now on live life as if someone of authority is standing and watching your every action. This is what it is like to live a life with integrity: when there is no difference between the actions of the public you and the actions of the private you.

From here forward, assume that all your actions are being observed by someone with authority — your mother or father, a police officer, your boss, your husband or wife, God, or whomever you "fear" most. This thought of always being watched should help guide your actions. There is no more "behind closed doors," "it's not illegal unless I get caught," or "what happens in Vegas stays in Vegas" kind of attitude about your life and the actions you take or the words you speak. Remember: behave as if someone is always watching you.

**Action Step 3: I will... Live Life with a Sense of Reality**

We experience life in the present through our Primitive Soul. Our Angelic Soul gives us the ability to comprehend past experiences and understand future possibilities. However, as human beings, we cannot live just in and for the present; that is for the animals. As human beings, we must live life knowing of our past experiences and knowing there is the possibility of a tomorrow's future.

Therefore, we must live life in the reality of knowing about the existence of a past, present, and future. All our decisions and actions need to be based on what is actually happening in the moment —

present time — with the proper influence of past experiences (lessons learned) and future desires (how we want life and the world to be).

This is the sense of reality we must live in. We must live in the realities of today. We cannot live in tomorrow — based on some "story" (scenarios) that we have made up in our head or based on wishful thinking or false beliefs. We cannot live in the past — based on some old memories or painful events. The past (history) is important to understand because it teaches us some very important lessons. Live life with a sense of reality — within the actual events that are occurring now.

**Action Step 4: I will... Take Care of My Body**

Our Primitive Soul and Angelic Soul interact with the reality of the physical world through our body; without a body, we could not interact with the material world. The body is the vehicle or conduit for our souls and the relationship among the three entities is synergistic. A body without its souls would have no human purpose for existing. This means our body has a sacred mission — it is the special vessel, the transport ship, of our Angelic Soul. For that reason, we must care for it so that our Angelic Soul can fulfill its purpose.

The health of our body has a direct effect on our Primitive Soul's and Angelic Soul's ability to interact and connect with the real world. So, it is in our best interest to keep the body we were given (considering of what we were born with or our DNA) in the best possible condition. We may not ask more from our body than we are willing to give, especially if we are abusing it. Caring for our body is accomplished through proper nourishment, activity, sleep, rest, respect, and treatment.

We have to be careful not to allow the overindulgences of our Primitive Soul's drive for immediate gratification in present time, limit the body's ability to function properly in the future. We need to control the Primitive Soul's drive for excess. The body is a sacred vessel, not a blank canvas, a pin cushion, or a liquor bottle. We really do not get to do with our body as our Primitive Soul motivates us without it suffering consequences. We must care for our body for our Angelic Soul's sake. The better the body is able to function, the better the Angelic Soul can motivate us to express our true self.

Proper nutrition, exercise, and rest are important. Spend more of your free time doing physical activities:

- Go for hikes
- Gardening
- Wash your car
- Take the stairs instead of the elevator or escalator

Find a nutrition program that works for you. Really experiment and find an exercise program that works for your body. Live for today, but workout and eat for tomorrow. Take care of your body — it is the one you have to live with.

**Action Step 5: I will... Simplify My Life**

It is time to give up our obsessions and compulsions. It is time to let go of our need to acquire stuff. This is our Primitive Soul in control of our life. Look at the different areas of your life, those places where you have too much (quantity and value). Greed is not an affliction of only the wealthy. Greed is a manifestation of an unchecked Primitive Soul drive to accumulate stuff in pursuit of abundance and prosperity. Rich or poor, we all have this Primitive Soul tendency toward greed.

We all have mental and physical baggage, stuff we have been carrying around for some time now. But now is the time to start unloading it. Excessive mental baggage could be our opinions, ideas, prejudices, and beliefs. Some of the worst mental baggage we carry around are our memories of bad, sad, and upsetting experiences.

Physical baggage is all the stuff we have accumulated. It is also our disproportionate need for physical beauty, with ourselves, our spouse, our children, our home, our car, and so forth. Look around your living and work spaces and be honest with yourself — do you have too much? This is your Primitive Soul driving you to physical abundance. But now is the time to take control and start shedding the unnecessary mental and physical excesses — say *no* to your Primitive Soul. Look around and simplify your life.

**Action Step 6: I will... Challenge Myself**

We cannot change and grow by remaining the same, thinking the same, or doing everything in the same ways. We need to have faith and courage to challenge ourselves to try new ways:

- Challenge yourself on how you care for your body (see action step 4).
- Challenge yourself on your identity issues. Identify which personal identity characteristics are holding you back from being happy and successful, then consider whether altering them can change who you are for the better. Remember, you cannot change and grow within your current identity; that is like a caged dog trying to be free to roam but being limited by the bars.
- Challenge yourself by committing to changing your mind on some issue — create flexibility and break out of being right all the time. Practice hearing others' side of the argument with an open mind, and then changing your mind; there are few universal truths.
- Challenge yourself in conversations to listen more and talk less. Ask more questions instead of giving answers. Have as your goal raising your empathy level — celebrate with others on their victories and listen to their stories without adding any of your own personal stories or anecdotes.
- Challenge yourself in giving more of yourself to others who could make use of your special skills and talents or just your time. Be open to helping others.

By challenging yourself, you will be pushing the envelope of your own physical and mental boundaries. You will be pleasantly surprised who you can become when you challenge yourself.

**Action Step 7: I will... Express My Sincere Gratitude, Appreciation, and Apology**

We do not go through life alone. Most of what we accomplish we do not accomplish alone. All kinds of people contribute to the quality of our life. Therefore, you need to acknowledge the people around you who are there helping you achieve by expressing your gratitude and appreciation for their help and contributions. But first you must be aware and understand that someone has done something for you in some way or another.

When we start noticing the little things that others do for us, their gifts to us, we can see that we need to express our gratitude and appreciation for each one. We can say "thank you," and this helps us connect with people by appreciating the little things they contribute to us, respecting them for their actions and words. A sincere "thank you" goes a long way in proving we care about those who enter our world.

When we ask someone for help, we can begin our request with "please." Remember, no one is obligated to do anything for you (and they are certainly not your slave). The Angelic Soul knows nothing of titles and positions, and therefore it sees all people as equals deserving of our gratitude and appreciation. Consider whatever help someone gives as their gift to you, so begin with "please" and end with "thank you."

The hardest words for us to express may be an apology, or "I'm sorry." An apology requires us first to admit to ourselves that we have done or said something wrong or improper and then to admit it to someone else. When we accept complete responsibility for our (good and bad) actions (refer to action step 1), apologizing for wrong or improper actions becomes easy, almost automatic. We can consider every apology for our wrong and improper acts as an opportunity to change and grow as a human being, not a threat to our Primitive Soul's existence, survival, or identity.

Whereas our Primitive Soul may be reluctant to express sincere gratitude, appreciation, or apology, our Angelic Soul may go overboard, to the point where it appears automatic or insincere. With proper soul flow, the necessary empathy and ability to relate to others will come to you. And with that raised level of empathy, you will be able to express sincere gratitude, appreciation, and apology.

**Action Step 8: I will... Set Aside Some Quiet Time**

Quiet time can also be known as "me time." Once a week, set aside some quiet time for yourself, even if it is as short as an hour. This quiet me time is personal and you can use it to connect with your Angelic Soul. Do something *for you*, not something *about you*, something for your body and your Angelic Soul; use this quiet time for yourself, but you do not need to do it alone.

An entire day of quiet time is ideal, but an hour is a good start. You do not have to spend the entire time on the same activity, but whichever activities you choose, make them be quiet-time activities:

- Solo sports (bicycling, walking, hiking, swimming)
- Yoga
- Painting or writing
- Reading a book
- Working on a hobby
- Getting in touch with nature
- Going to religious or spiritual services

In addition, during this quiet time "unplug." Let your mind fill with your thoughts, not with music or other forms of electronic chatter; quiet time is thinking time and time to interact with yourself and engage your Angelic Soul to express itself in thought, creativity, learning, or other such activities.

**Action Step 9: I will... Share Something of Myself**

Believe it or not, the world does not revolve around you and your life alone. Just as we want others to contribute to our needs, we in turn need to contribute to others by sharing something of ourselves. This is not about only giving money. It is about putting ourselves out there in the world, participating in the world, and, more importantly, contributing to the world (our family and community).

Sharing something of yourself with others involves giving your time, a special skill, or talent that you have — your gift:

- Speak kind words — even as simple as "hello," "good morning," and "thank you"
- Hold the door for someone

- Be the special person in someone else's life
- Be a leader, mentor, or a teacher for some youth group
- Spend time with family and friends
- Do volunteer work for a hospital or charity

We can learn how to help others without feeling the need to justify doing so; we do it just because it is the right thing to do. It is not about doing it to feel good about ourselves. If we feel better afterward, that does not change the fact it is still the right thing to do. Get out of your comfort zone and go share something of yourself with the world.

**Action Step 10: I will... Find, Define, and Act on My Purpose**

Working on this action step activates your Angelic Soul and brings direction to some of the other action steps. We each must find some purpose (a project, an activity, or a passion) that engages the motivation of our Angelic Soul for a purpose that is bigger than us as individuals. Look around your life and find a purpose that is emotionally "close to home." Your purpose will not be handed to you; it is your task alone to discover and

> *"There are no extra human beings; you are on this Earth to do something special with your life."*
> Brian Tracy

wrestle it out from hiding. Find a purpose that piques your interest, that brings meaning and direction to your life, that makes your life worth living. Your purpose could be one big one or multiple smaller ones:

- Create a foundation to address a worldly problem
- Work to become a caring and loving spouse
- Work to become a caring, loving, and involved parent
- Become the special someone that others come to depend on for their happiness or success

More than just giving of yourself, your purpose also involves something you own and have a passion for, something that moves you to action. You cannot discover your purpose unless you know how and where to look. So, talk with people or search out organizations that are engaged in activities that serve the greater good. What is important here is that the projects or activities really touch your Angelic Soul.

Do not search for the perfect purpose; instead, act on what comes up and let your purpose evolve and change along the way. Make as much of your daily actions part of your purpose as you can. Define your purpose so that it is very clear to you what it is and how it brings meaning to your life, and then make the time and effort to act on your purpose, to bring it to life so that in return your purpose brings life to you.

**Action Step 11: I will... Be the Example for Others to Follow**

We all need mentors in our life, someone we look to for guidance and teaching. Now that someone is you. Whether or not you actually create that formal and defined relationship with someone is not the issue. You need to know that wherever you go someone may be there looking up to you as the example to follow (even if you do not notice that someone is watching your every action). Therefore, set the example in your life for others to follow. Combined with action step 6, this action step will change your world.

Whereas action step 2 is about acting with integrity even when no one is watching, this action step is about creating higher standards for all to see. This action step is about being accountable to others, standing higher, reaching past the lowest-common denominator. Be the best — not at everything, but at some things.

People, especially children and other heavily Primitive Soul-motivated people, will do half of what you say and twice of what you do. Stop wishing for others to change until you do — lead by example. Be that person you would want others to duplicate:

- Be the husband you want your son to be.
- Be the wife you want your daughter to be.
- Be the best of friends.
- Be the leader you would want to follow.
- Be the person that you can count on 24/7.

Whatever you want to see in the world — peace, friendship, forgiveness, involvement, charity — you need to be it first and set the example for others to follow.

**Action Step 12: I will... Count My Blessings**
Finally, during the quiet time you regularly set aside (see action step 8), count your blessings — all those gifts you receive each day. Blessings may be the direct result of our own efforts or actions or something we had no part in making happen.

Start the accounting of your blessings by acknowledging gratitude for these gifts, and then add any others that have affected your life in a positive manner:

- Gift of life: Appreciate and be thankful that you had one more day or week on Earth to accomplish your life purpose, to bring joy, happiness, friendship, and love into the lives of the people around you, and to bring positive change and influence to the people in your life.
- Gift of love: Acknowledge all the people you love and who love the person you are and the person you can become and those who are there for you unconditionally.
- Gift of family: Express gratitude for your family and express appreciation for their being in your life and how they contribute to your happiness.
- Gift of friendship: Appreciate the people who bring camaraderie, peace, joy, and companionship to your life.
- Gift of abundance: Acknowledge your job (or whatever provides you with a source of income or livelihood), the food on your table, the roof over your head, the car(s) in your driveway, and the toys in your garage; be grateful for all the tangible and intangible things that bring material happiness to your life.
- Gift of possibility: Appreciate the opportunity to bring change to yourself, your family, your community, and the world.

Amid the chaos and activity of your life, the most important thing is to be grateful for the life you were granted this morning when you woke up. Without the ability to *live* life today, you do not have the opportunity to fulfill your life purpose. Each day on Earth, we are given one more chance to do the right things — to turn our life around and to make some positive impact on the world. Say to yourself each morning, "This is a new day with new opportunities for making a difference in my life and in someone else's life." And remember to count your blessings each day; regardless of the quantity, just focus on the quality of each gift.

## *Key Takeaways*

1. Post these twelve action steps all around your environment for you to see each and every day:
   - I will... Own My Life
   - I will... Live Life as If Someone Is Always Watching
   - I will... Live Life with a Sense of Reality
   - I will... Take Care of My Body
   - I will... Simplify My Life
   - I will... Challenge Myself
   - I will... Express My Sincere Gratitude, Appreciation, and Apology
   - I will... Set Aside Some Quiet Time
   - I will... Share Something of Myself
   - I will... Find, Define, and Act on My Purpose
   - I will... Be the Example for Others to Follow
   - I will... Count My Blessings
2. Follow the action step process to implement the twelve action steps:
   - Want to change.
   - Incorporate the twelve action steps.
   - Review actions and results.
   - Reenact your actions.

# ACHIEVING A BETTER LIFE

*Ninety per cent of the world's woe comes from people not knowing themselves, their abilities, their frailties, and even their real virtues. Most of us go almost all the way through life as complete strangers to ourselves—so how can we know anyone else?*
—Sydney J. Harris, American journalist

THANK YOU FOR TAKING THIS journey with me into the mind, body, and soul of our human nature. Now the first big step of the journey into our human nature has come to the end of the beginning. In Section 2, we discovered a new way of seeing who we are as human beings — those unique characteristics about human nature that set us apart from the animals and that drive our actions and reactions. We started by reverse engineering the human being, taking our humanity apart, examining it, and understanding its constituent parts, which led us to recognize the existence of the body, the existence of the Primitive Soul and the Angelic Soul (that comprise the internal Human Operating System), and the complete Human Control System (the overall operational model of the human being that encompasses the body and the internal Human Operating System[48]). Reverse

---

48 internal Human Operating System (iHOS) — a system that describes how human nature operates as driven by our Primitive Soul and our Angelic Soul; it operates within our body to animate our body.

engineering of the human being leads to an equation that describes it in its simplest form:

Human Being = Body + Souls

= Body + [$x$%PS + (100% − $x$%) × AS]

where: PS is the Primitive Soul

AS is the Angelic Soul

$x$% = 0 to 100% time spent in Primitive Soul, and

(100% − $x$%) is the remaining time spent in the Angelic Soul

The Human Control System operational model is relatively simple (as shown in Figure 9), and yet it can explain our seemingly complex (and sometimes confusing) human nature. The Human Control System operational model of the human condition gives us a better understanding of who we are as human beings, what drives and motivates us to do and say the things we do and say. You have now learned something new (something you did not know you did not know), so it is time to create a new knowledge bucket for the internal Human Operating System and the Human Control System (see Figure 26).

**Figure 26. New iHOS and HCS knowledge bucket.**

People who say life and people are complicated say that to maintain some level of mystery and control over us or the situation. Any situation can be broken down into smaller, simpler parts, and each part can then be examined and understood, which creates a better understanding of the entire situation (without the Primitive

Soul drama of "it's too complicated"). The complication goes away and the situation can be understood in total. Our internal Human Operating System is simple once we understand the parts and details of the Human Control System operational model and the motivations of our Primitive Soul and our Angelic Soul.

## I'm Only Human

Human beings are created or have evolved to be perfect by design — a body plus a Primitive Soul plus an Angelic Soul. It is our actions that are imperfect. It is the way in which we execute the plan that is imperfect. Being human, are actions are not perfect — get over it. Being human is a challenge brought about by having a two-part soul, and that must be by design.

So, we can ask again, "Is human nature a blessing or a curse?" and "Is 'I'm only human' an excuse or a justification?" We now know the answer to these questions is, "It depends." It depends on you. It depends on how YOU look at it and how YOU deal with it. If you choose to understand and embrace our human nature for what it is, then it will look more like a blessing, providing us with many freedoms. Ignore the details and motivations of our human nature, and it will most certainly continue to be a curse, a trap of automated responses and poor results.

"I'm only human" is not an excuse or a bad thing. Human nature is a condition, a condition of life. Work in concert with our human nature and achieve harmony with yourself and others. Ignore our human nature and produce stress, chaos, and failure. When presented with two options, choose the one that creates the greatest opportunity for change and growth. Play or be played — either we learn to understand our human nature, or other people or circumstances around us will use human nature to control us. When we neglect to consider the natural order of things, we will fail.

## Courage to Change

It is hardest to focus change and growth on our personal issues, because they directly involve YOU, and we are resistant to change, bad or good. It is way easier to point the finger at someone else (that could be a spouse, children, coworkers) and say, "You change; you need to be better," and avoid the three other fingers pointing back. This reminds me of a story. I was once asked, "Why do I need to change?" My reply was, "Because me changing and being a better person does not make you a better person — because me changing will not change you." People usually expect more of others than they do of themselves that is also our human nature:

> *"Everyone thinks of changing the world, but no one thinks of changing himself."*
> Leo Tolstoy

- We fight for peace in the world, but we will not make peace with our own family.
- We say to others, "You do as I say, not as I do." All talk, but we do not set the example for others to follow.
- We can dish it out, but we can't take it. We are harder on others than we are on ourselves and we take ourselves too seriously.

Change and growth must start at home — our home. We all need to change and grow to some extent or another. However, just know that the ones we think need it the most (more than us) will not see it that way. They believe they do not need to change or grow. The only answer to this dilemma is you do your own changing and growing for you (it is your gift to all who know you) and move on without them. Change and grow for yourself, not for anyone else. Take responsibility for and ownership of your own

> *"You must take personal responsibility. You cannot change the circumstances, the seasons, or the wind, but you can change yourself. That is something you have charge of."*
> Jim Rohn

life, your own human nature, your own actions, and your own results and successes.

Remember, change cannot occur through our Primitive Soul. Our Primitive Soul is comfortable with the routine (comfort zone), and it does not like change. Our Angelic Soul is driven to be creative. And when our Angelic Soul motivates us to be creative, we are then open to the opportunity of change. Creativity, innovation, and change all go hand in hand.

Accountability and responsibility open the gateway to change and growth. There is no excuse for not taking responsibility for our life. Without accountability and responsibility, we cannot (or will not) look at what needs to change so that we can make better decisions and have better relationships in the future. Future happiness comes with change and growth in the present. The world cannot be a better place unless people understand this and make a real attempt at changing, improving, and growing.

When I say you need to operate to "serve the greater good," I mean YOU need to operate to serve the greater good. This information is *not* for you to use against someone else. This information is for you to change your world around you, starting with "being the change you want to see in the world." This information is for you personally, not some other person. You need to perform the acts of "serve the greater good." It is about YOU choosing in the moment whether to act from your Primitive Soul (and its "all about me" motivation) or from your Angelic Soul (and its "serve the greater good" motivation). You need to make the decisions about being a better son or daughter, sister or brother, husband or wife, mother or father, boss, employee, or human being and you need to have the courage to follow through and take on the challenges of our human nature, not be controlled by it like some puppet on a string.

> *"Courage is the first of the human qualities because it is a quality which guarantees all the others."*
> Winston Churchill

# Clarity

Once you begin to assimilate this newfound knowledge of the internal Human Operating System and the Human Control System, along with the twelve action step adjustments, you will begin to see yourself and others in your world a lot differently — with clarity and understanding. To some degree, this is unfortunate because you will want others to change as you do. You must contain yourself and try to be calm with your new sense of clarity. You may not use the information you have learned to make someone else change. This information is only for you; it is here for you to use to change and grow. Others need to find their own path to discovering their human nature.

Do not use this information as a stick to hit others over the head with. It will not work. Just like you, they need to be willing to absorb the information and create and fill their own knowledge bucket with it. In addition, you are not allowed to use this information against anyone to manipulate or guilt trip them into doing something or to make them feel bad about themselves (that will be your Primitive Soul at work).

The objective of this book is to wake up the Angelic Soul motivations within you, because when we predominately live out of our Primitive Soul we live among the herd, just like any other sheep. Knowing all this new information produces an improved you. From here forward, you are no longer the same person.

Here is the catch if you choose not to understand your human nature:

- You do not ever stand a chance of understanding others, and without understanding them, you cannot be in a true relationship with them.
- Others who do understand can and will use it to exploit our human nature against us.
- You will continue your life on automatic pilot, with no free will and no free choice, repeating the same mistakes over and over again.

- You will live a life with no empathy, no compassion, no love, lots of anger, and many miscommunications.
- You will continue to live only worrying about today and living only for yourself.

## Choose Who You Are Going to Be

Honesty — the first person you must be honest with is yourself in admitting *you need to change* (a little or a lot, it does not matter). You really need to be honest with yourself about all things. *Until you are honest with yourself, it is impossible for others to be honest with you.*

Integrity — live so that your actions are consistent with your words, and your words are consistent with your actions.

The first person you need to learn how to be in an open and honest relationship with is you. Be honest with yourself and be willing to hear the truth about yourself. Do what is necessary to learn the real you so you can disconnect the *way* you are from the *who* you are. Only your cobbled-together, made-up Primitive Soul identity is at risk, not your life. Be the genuine you; do not take the easy way just because it is easy.

Look at your identity and each of your personal identity characteristics as key determiners of your future success. Now you get to decide who you are and what you are going to allow to define you. Remember, our Primitive Soul-motivated identity is the *way* we are; our Angelic Soul will direct us to *who* we really are.

> *"We cannot become what we need to be by remaining what we are."*
> Max DePree

Learn how to adapt who you are to different circumstances and situations. There is an appropriate time and place for everything (our Primitive Soul or our Angelic Soul and which personal identity characteristic we show). Here are two important thoughts:

1) There is a big difference between what we *want* to hear and what we *need* to hear. Listen closely for what you *need* to hear. Do not shut it out because it is too hard to listen to.

2) Just because you can does not mean you should. I have heard oh so many times, "I have the right to" do this, that, and the other thing. "It is my body; I'll do with it what I want." Just because you have the *ability* does not automatically give you the permission or the right. Look carefully at whether it is your Primitive Soul or your Angelic Soul driving your decisions and choices.

## Choice and Consequences

Each of our life's choices has results and consequences. In general, most of what we have in life (income, relationships, success, and so on) is a result of where we started and the decisions and choices that we made along the way; different choices lead to different outcomes. Those

> *"Your present circumstances don't determine where you can go; they merely determine where you start."*
> Nido Qubein

who choose wisely and responsibly have a far greater likelihood of success, whereas those who choose foolishly and irresponsibly have a far greater likelihood of failure. Most often in life, our destination is determined by the course we have taken based on the decisions we have made.

The simple Law of the Harvest — "as you sow, so shall you reap" — sometimes is applied as "the harder you work, the more you get out of it." When all is said and done, in the end, *you need to decide which is more important to you: who you are now or who you want to be.* And today is the day to start making the changes and

> *"The best time to plant a tree was twenty years ago. The second best time is today."*
> Chinese proverb

growing toward a better future. If you have gotten this far and you do not see how any of this applies to you, then you definitely missed it. You need to start over and try harder.

## In Conclusion

Clearly, human beings have come a long way technologically from the early days of sticks and stones, but from a humanistic standpoint, not so far. There is still hunger, hatred, and killing in the world, and lots of unhappy people walking the planet. War, hate, prejudice, and all the other negative things will not end as long as people live Primitive Soul-motivated lives. You may not think *you* need to change and grow, but the world[49] certainly does need to change — one person at a time — and you need to change and grow for the sake of the world. We do not get to push the need to change the world off on someone else, some charitable organization we donate to, or (worst yet) the government. Now is the time for you to make the necessary changes in your life to live more from your Angelic Soul and in this way to create a better future; otherwise, we can look to our past and humanity's past and not expect a much different future. And do not worry; our Primitive Soul will always be there to take care of our bodily needs regardless of how much we focus on our Angelic Soul's goals.

There is what we think (internal) and how we act (external) — both are who we are. *Thinking* is the struggle between our Primitive Soul and our Angelic Soul, and *acting* is the result of which soul wins. We cannot ever turn off our Primitive Soul; but, we can allow our Angelic Soul greater opportunity to influence our lives.

Never take the power of human nature for granted, even though most people can keep their negative issues under control in "normal" circumstances. Human nature has not evolved away — so do not create a rosy view of the world and act as if it has. Wanting to believe everyone is an Angelic Soul is naive.

---

49 The world — this includes your spouse, family, job/company, community, and, lastly, the rest of the planet.

The big problem with our Primitive Soul is that it motivates us to do things on our own. The Primitive Soul is not a team player. It strives to stand on its own, to do it its own way. This Primitive Soul characteristic of human beings leads us to reinventing ourselves in each new generation. A new generation starts off by putting down previous generations as uninformed, backward, or old-fashioned. The new generation always claims to know better than previous generations. And then after years of experience and hard-learned lessons, it arrives at where the previous generation stood, wondering what happened, and discovering that their parents and ancestors were not that stupid. With this kind approach to life, human beings may advance technologically, but not humanistically. To make progress from a humanistic viewpoint (to create a future of peace and prosperity), human beings must start by learning from the best and wisest of earlier generations. Future generations must stand on the shoulders of the giants who came before them to create a future we are all dreaming of.

> *"If I have seen further than others, it is by standing upon the shoulders of giants."*
> Isaac Newton

Very, very few human beings are perfect. Many, many generations may pass before even one perfect human being surfaces. We simply cannot stand around and wait. Though few are perfect, many are wise and offer much to learn from. And though few are perfect or wise, we all can still push to be better human beings and to reach beyond the negative aspects of our Primitive Soul motivations.

The key to our happiness and success in life is soul flow — the ability to present our Primitive Soul and Angelic Soul at the appropriate time and place. Nurturing our Primitive Soul is the key to prosperity; nurturing our Angelic Soul is the key to life-long happiness. If you want both prosperity and happiness, you need to develop your soul flow. Be conscious of the influences and motivations your Primitive Soul and Angelic Soul have on you all the time. Feed your Angelic Soul so that it will bring you more meaning, peace, and love in your life.

Whether or not a Primitive Soul and an Angelic Soul actually exist within us, take it on faith for right now, because it does affect our daily lives whether we care to understand or accept it or not. Whether we believe in them or not, the internal Human Operating System and the Human Control System operational model predicts our human nature, and that is what is important and, when understood and used properly, provides us the opportunity of a better life, for you and all the people around you. Try this out for a while and see what happens. The choice is all yours. Thank you for allowing me to share with you this new perspective on human nature. I hope it changes your life for the better, as it did mine.

> *"Though no one can go back and make a brand new start, anyone can start from now and make a brand new ending."*
> Carl Bard

## *Key Takeaways*

1. The relatively simple internal Human Operating System and Human Control System operational model of the human condition gives us a better understanding of who we are as human beings.

2. Whether human nature is a blessing or a curse and whether "I'm only human" is an excuse or a justification all depends on how YOU look at it and how YOU deal with it. Work in concert with our human nature and achieve harmony with yourself and others. Ignore our human nature and produce stress, chaos, and failure.

3. You need to decide to be a better person and you need to have the courage to follow through and take on the challenges of our human nature (and not be controlled by it).

4. You will begin to see yourself and others in your world a lot differently from how you did before. But you may not use the information you have just learned to make someone else change or feel guilty.

5. You need to be honest with yourself and be willing to hear the truth about yourself.

6. You need to look at your identity and each of your personal identity characteristics as key determiners of your future success. Decide who you are and what you are going to allow to define you, now and into the future.

7. You need to decide which is more important to you: who you are now or who you want to be in the future.

8. Our life's choices have results and consequences. Choose wisely and responsibly and you will have a far greater likelihood of success.

9. You need to live each day thinking about which soul you are going to feed that day — the "all about me" Primitive Soul or the "serve the greater good" Angelic Soul. The choice is all yours and it is very important to choose wisely and freely.

10. Do not wait for a better day or for your life to get worse to start. There is no better time than now! Commit and get started. No one can do it for you, but you.

11. To be a better human being, three things must happen:
    - You must want to be a *different person* (a lot or a little), as much as you have ever wanted anything.
    - You must be willing to *take the path* in that direction each day.
    - You must be *accepting of the truth* (about yourself and your human nature).

And to my father's favorite saying, I add the following:
"If there's a will, there's a way.
But if there's a whine, there's a delay."

# ACKNOWLEDGMENTS

There are many people I would like and need to thank for their help, input, and support in the writing of this book, starting with my good friend Dr. David Lichtman (of blessed memory), with whom I discussed the basics of this subject matter early on. You led me to a real breakthrough when you challenged me to look at this subject matter from an engineering perspective. So, I did, and then when I combined it with my studies of Kabbalah and other religious subjects (to give it the spiritual element); this is what I came up with, and for that, I thank you very much.

To my friend Ben Heyman, my first-draft reviewer and guinea pig, you gave me clarity on how the subject matter was reaching people. As I wrote, you were always waiting for the next chapter to read; you called the material your "crack." Thank you so much for your constant feedback and commitment as I wrote each chapter.

To my colleague from Rocketdyne Dr. Dale S. Deardorff, Director of Innovation and Strategic Thinking at the Rocky Peak Leadership Center (www.rockypeaklc.com), I appreciate you taking your time to read the first completed draft of the book and for all your insightful feedback on its content. Your specific suggestion to include personal exercises as a method for readers to get a deeper understanding of the material led to the addition of the Exercise Breaks. These personal interactions with the material in the book will be extremely useful to all the readers.

And, most definitely, to the hundreds and maybe thousands of people I observed over the course of the years that it took to finally write this book, I thank you for all your humanity and the display of your human nature as I captured your interactions and validated the theories within the book. Your human nature was truly an inspiration.

To my children, Marisa and Daniel, you have brought a purpose to my life. You are a parent's dream come true. Thank you both for being who you are. But most of all, to my wife, Sharon, a true Angelic Soul and a yin to my yang, your constant love and support are immeasurable. The fact that I have finished writing this book is only because of who you are in my life, and for that, I will be eternally grateful.

*"A real man loves his wife, and places his family as*
*the most important thing in life. Nothing has*
*brought me more peace and content in life than*
*simply being a good husband and father."*
Frank Abagnale

# BOOK NOTES


**References:**
"I'm Only Human," The Jewish Woman; Chabad.

Chapter 1

"Index of Major Conflicts since 1700," WorldStatesmen.org, www.worldstatesmen.org.

Maria, "10 Wars Throughout History That Left Behind Devastating Death Tolls," History Collection, http://historycollection.co/10-wars-throughout-history-left-behind-devastating-death-tolls/10/.

Chapter 2

Alpha High IQ Society, http://www.iq-test.net/iq-test-famous-people.html.

"Famous IQ," Listal, http://www.listal.com/list/famous-iq.

Kayla Marie Walsh, "10 Famous People With Surprisingly High IQs," The Richest, http://www.therichest.com/rich-list/most-shocking/10-famous-people-with-surprisingly-high-iqs/.

Stephen, "IQ Facts and IQ of Famous People," Interesting Facts, http://academictips.org/interesting-facts/iq-facts-and-iq-of-famous-people/.

Chapter 4

Jim H, "Weighing Human Souls—the 21 Grams Theory," Historic Mysteries, http://www.historicmysteries.com/the-21-gram-soul-theory/.

**Figure Sources:**

Figure 2 — A.C.E. Intelligence website, http://www.aceintelligence.com

# ABOUT THE AUTHOR

Norbert Soski earned his Bachelor of Science in Electrical Engineering at the University of Southern California. After completing his degree, he started his engineering career designing hand-held electronic games at Mattel Electronics, division of Mattel Toys and holds a patent on one (www. handheldmuseum.com/ Mattel/LAGames.htm).

Norbert then moved on to designing computer and avionics systems for such programs as the F-16 LANTIRN pod and MILSTAR satellite, the electrical power system for the International Space Station (ISS), rocket engine control systems for the Delta IV RS-68 first-stage engine and J-2X upper-stage engine, and environmental control systems for industrial kitchen equipment. As an engineer, Norbert really enjoys creating products that have never existed before. His greatest professional achievement was the RS-68 Engine Control Unit; a first of its kind rocket engine controller.

In addition to his many years of technical and engineering studies and experiences, Norbert has spent many years informally studying religion, forms of spiritualism, and Kabbalah. Norbert is the founder of Straight-Up Soulutions (www.SUSoulutions.com), a consulting and coaching company — focused on finding solutions to problems based on our internal Human Operating System (iHOS) — for both individuals and companies. In his off time, he mostly enjoys bicycling, along with launching high-powered model rockets out in the desert.

# APPENDIX

## Soul Characteristics Summary & Comparison

THE PRIMITIVE SOUL AND THE Angelic Soul each have a unique and specific set of key characteristics. These key characteristics describe how each soul in the internal Human Operating System operates and responds to life's many events (see Table 8).

**Table 8. Comparison of Key Soul Characteristics**

| Characteristic | Primitive Soul | Angelic Soul |
|---|---|---|
| Purpose | Runs the body's basic and involuntary functions | Connects with other souls (relationships) and the universe |
| Objectives | Survive<br><br>Eating, reproducing, protection of self, security, indulging in bodily needs<br><br>Indulging in self | Thrive<br><br>Freedom, learning, and growing, happiness, love, purpose<br><br>Relationships |
| Connection | Directly to the body | To the infinite and the universe |
| Time Frame | Now, present time | Past and future |
| Lifetime | One-time — precious, short | Forever — always a next time |
| Action | Doing, then thinking<br><br>Instinct | Thinking, then doing<br><br>Intuitive |

| Characteristic | Primitive Soul | Angelic Soul |
|---|---|---|
| Action Response | Automatic for involuntary functions, pain response (no thought involved), learned and trained responses | Calculated, logical, thought-through, voluntary responses |
| Human Reference | Looks and operates inside the body, "I" or "me," looks out for self | Looks and operates outside the body |
| Potential | Limited to the body and present time<br><br>Constant, absolute, inflexible, fixed, resists change, regimented, habits, rut, routine, does what it always does, inertia | Practically unlimited (by human standards)<br><br>Open to learning and growth, choices and options, flexible and adaptable, creative |
| Vision | Sees the world as an illusion, random, impersonal, and a threat to the body and safety | Sees a future; drives to create and learn, hope, love, and compassion |
| Right and Wrong | Needs laws, rules, and boundaries to keep order; conflicts between what is right for self versus what is right for group and society | Inherent knowledge of what is right and wrong for self and society |
| Catchphrase | "It's all about me"<br>"What's in it for me" | "Serve the greater good" |
| Ultimate Goal | Drive for personal pleasure and satisfaction<br><br>Does what *feels or looks good* now, but does not necessarily *do good* for the long-term | Seeks out a "greater purpose" for living, contributes to the universe, love, long-term prosperity and happiness<br><br>Does what *does good* for now and into the future |

| Characteristic | Primitive Soul | Angelic Soul |
| --- | --- | --- |
| Motivational Factors | Abundance and Prosperity<br>Pain and Pleasure<br>Identity and Belonging | Purpose and Meaning<br>Knowledge and Creativity<br>Peace and Love |
| Moves Away From | Pain | Confusion |
| Moves Toward | Pleasure, self-indulgence | Peace, love, freedom |
| What the Soul Enjoys from Life | Sex, profit and gain, fame and recognition, bigger and better | Creativity (art, music, literature), spirituality, intimacy, and love |
| Soul One Human Being to Another | All the same; but drives for unique identity<br>(herd, sheep) | Each is different; unique person to person |
| Emotions | Fear, envy | Love, joy |
| Feelings | Stressed, worried | Calm, peaceful |
| Give & Take Exchange Cycle | Taking<br>Selfishness<br>Does not share — "what is mine is mine"<br>Will give only if it directly benefits some other motivational factor<br>"I want, I want, I want" | Giving<br>Sacrifice<br>Shares willingly, sometimes to an extreme — "what is mine is yours"<br>Will take reluctantly |
| Trust | Starts with the assumption "I do not trust you, even if there is no previous evidence not to trust you"<br>Always skeptical of others' motives<br>People are not to be trusted; they are all in it for themselves<br>"You must earn my trust"<br>Trust is an elusive target | Starts with unverified faith in people and sometimes is caught trusting the wrong people<br><br>"You have my trust until you lose it" |